swinging the billy

Indigenous and other styles of Australian bush cooking

Kingsley Palmer

Aboriginal Studies Press
1999

First published in 1999 by Aboriginal Studies Press for the Australian Institute of Aboriginal and Torres Strait Islander Studies, GPO Box 553, Canberra, ACT 2601.

National Library of Australia Cataloguing-in-Publication Data:

    Palmer, Kingsley, 1946-
      Swinging the Billy

    ISBN 0 85575 317 X

    1. Cookery, Australian. 2. Cookery (Wild foods).
    3. Aborigines, Australian - Food. 4. Outdoor cookery. I.

    641.5994

Produced by Aboriginal Studies Press
Designed by design ONE Solutions
Printed in Australia by Goanna Print

Acknowledgments

I wish to thank the many people who shared their recipes and their meals with me, taught me their skills and savoured my cooking. Bush cooking is a tradition and, like all traditions, it is passed on through custom and practice, by word of mouth and by observation. I thank all who contributed to my knowledge over the years and I hope that this little book does their wisdom justice.

In particular, I thank the many Indigenous people with whom I worked and who so generously showed me their culinary culture, patiently explained the complex and often intricate cooking and food preparation methods, and always encouraged me to try things.

Thanks go to the Australian Institute of Aboriginal and Torres Strait Islander Studies (AIATSIS) which provided practical support to enable me to produce this book.

I also thank Warwick Dix, who first introduced me to the Australian bush and showed me how to look after myself in odd spots; Clancy McKenna who taught me many bush skills; Charles Hamilton, Don McCaskill, Kim Akerman, Kim Barber, Maggie Brady, all of whom added to my knowledge of bush cooking and who, in various ways, contributed to this volume. I thank the editors and staff of Aboriginal Studies Press for their advice and support and in particular Elysebeth Fraser-Price. I also thank David Horton for helpful comments on an earlier draft of this book. Finally, I thank my wife, Di Hosking, for the many helpful suggestions that greatly improved both the form and content of what follows and for the typically Australian dictum with which the Introduction starts.

I have done my best to identify correctly those who appear in the photographs used in this book. All photographs were taken with the permission of those appearing in them. In a few cases I regret that I have been unable to identify some individuals and my apologies go to those whose names have not been acknowledged.

Disclaimer

Some of the animals and animal products included in these recipes are protected species or by-products of protected species. They can be taken only by those Indigenous people who are permitted by law to hunt them for personal consumption.

Warning

Care should be taken if using this cookbook in Aboriginal communities as it may contain photographs of deceased people. If you have any doubt about using this book in such circumstances always consult with the community elders first.

contents

Introduction 7

Bush Kitchen 11

Utensils 11

Water 15

Camp site 17

Fire 17

Wind 21

Protection of the natural environment 22

And other things… 24

Indigenous Bush Recipes 27

Non-Indigenous Styles of Australian Bush Cooking 51

And To Finish — Liqueur and an After-dinner Mint 72

Index 75

Recipes 77

introduction

Who called the cook a bastard?
Who called the bastard a cook!

Various books have been written about bush cooking in Australia. They represent many different approaches but many have two common themes:

> you can eat gourmet food in the bush; and
> you can luxuriate in home comforts.

Having spent countless nights in the Australian bush since my first encounter with it over twenty-five years ago I'm a little sceptical about these claims. Much depends on the resources you have available. If you think you can cart a gas stove, sink, electric mixer, fridge, generator, table, chairs and caviar on ice with the best crystal, then of course, it could be just like home.

But how practical is this on rough dirt roads, or no roads at all, when the temperature is 40°C plus, the flies swarm and the dust penetrates everything? Not very, believe me. It's a matter of doing the best you can, of using appropriate equipment and employing methods that are suitable for difficult circumstances. This means that some things just have to be left behind. But with ingenuity and good planning its surprising how comfortable you can be and how well you can eat.

This is a cookbook about practicalities. It is designed for people who want to experience the wonders of the bush but who do not have a mobile home (let alone a mobile 'phone) and a legion of expensive equipment to go with it. It is written for people who want to be reasonably comfortable in the bush and who want to eat good food which is easy to prepare using utensils and ingredients that can be carried in difficult conditions.

Another slightly different type of bush cooking — catering to the needs of the bush walker and rock climber — emphasises the need for light gear and the innovation of so called 'lite' food. Complex utensils made of space-age alloys and cookers that weigh almost nothing are part of this tradition. Dehydrated 'meat', nuts and dried fruit, with little water and no tins constitute a diet for those wishing to travel on foot to remote places. While some of the recipes and information in this book will be useful to people who want to travel light, for the most part, these recipes are for the vehicularly mobile. For most of these recipes you will need a substantial fire with plenty of hot coals and a billy or pot designed to fit a truck back rather than a backpack.

My work over the last twenty-five years has involved much contact with Indigenous Australians, the first owners of the Australian continent. They have much to teach us about living in and off the bush as well as about diverse ways of preparing food, little appreciated or understood by most Australians. The Indigenous material included here is largely drawn from the remoter areas of Australia. It represents, for the most part, ways of cooking and preparing food that are slight modifications of traditional practice. Some have remained unchanged since before the arrival of Europeans. Readers unfamiliar with the diversity of cultures within Indigenous Australia, should note that by far the majority of Australia's original owners now prepare their food in circumstances and using methods identical to most other Australians. I make this statement simply to avoid any stereotyping and misunderstanding on the part of those unfamiliar with Australia who might be misled into believing that traditional practice remains the only practice for Aboriginal and Torres Strait Islander peoples in Australia today.

It is important to note that some of these recipes use Indigenous ingredients that derive from species that are protected by law and therefore cannot be used by non-Indigenous people. I will return to this issue later.

I start with some basics: the hearth, the apparatus and the cooking utensils.

With some very basic items and some skill and care, you can set yourself up very nicely and enjoy good food, which is well prepared and a pleasure to eat.

The first part of this cookbook contains traditional Indigenous Australian recipes, described in detail, that I have collected over the years. It is by no means an exhaustive list and Indigenous Australians have many additional recipes not included here. However, the selection provides a good cross-section of the recipes employed by Indigenous people. I also include some anecdotes to fill in the time while the fire burns down or the kangaroo cools.

The second part is written for all bush cooks. I have attempted to provide practical, tasty and easy-to-prepare dishes. Some are simply adaptations of meals you can prepare at home. Others are more specific to the bush and the particular circumstances of camping out.

Breakfast in the bush is best kept simple. Who wants to eat bacon and eggs before a long day on the rough corrugated track: or to spend the day in the confines of a hot Toyota cab with someone who ate kippers for breakfast?

Only a few dessert recipes are provided reflecting my view that meals outback and under the stars are best kept simple. Two or three courses will be too much for most people's logistical resources, let alone their arteries.

Enjoy reading, enjoy travelling in the Australian bush and, above all, enjoy eating. After all, these are three of the great pleasures of life.

I once spent three weeks with only a Swiss army knife and a mug on a trip in the Great Sandy Desert south of Balgo in Western Australia. I carved a wooden 'spoon' which I used to eat and managed for the most part. I don't recommend this approach. It was simple and efficient in terms of space and cost but eating was never a pleasure and the mug became so disgusting that even the camp dogs shunned it.

bush kitchen

Before we move into the serious business of cooking and eating, it will be helpful to discuss briefly some of the paraphernalia you may require. I once watched a now quite eminent bushy unload literally everything, including a kitchen sink, from the back of his Landrover. With the increased frequency and length of my bush trips I found that I needed fewer gadgets and less equipment which lightened the load considerably. However, a few pieces of basic equipment are essential for good cooking.

Utensils

The basic rule about utensils is this:

The more you have, the more you need and the more difficult they are to keep clean.

You need enough to make life comfortable but not so many that chores become unbearable.

Billy can

Many of the Indigenous people in remote communities with whom I worked use the minimum of utensils preferring to cook directly on the open fire. They all, however, in my experience use the humble billy can, or billy, and usually a camp oven or large saucepan.

The billy appears to have its origins in the Scottish *bally*, a milk-pail; just as well to know the origins of an essential item that is synonymous with the very essence of bush life.

When you buy a billy can it usually has a lid. Get rid of it. The problem with lids is that, when the billy gets bent, and it will, the lid won't fit or it will stick on and you will burn yourself trying to get it off. Many billies are made of aluminium which will melt on a really hot fire, and aluminum is possibly bad for your health in any case. Some billies are

Always look for ways to cook that involve little or no washing up. Not only is washing up a chore but, if water is scarce, it can be impracticable.

11

To make a billy

Remove the rim of the tin with a tin opener. Using fencing wire or an old coat hanger, fashion a longish wire handle and fasten it through holes pierced in the top of the tin just below the rim. The wire should be long enough so that the top of the handle remains cool and above the flames.

designed to nest and fit inside one another which means that the charcoal from one grinds into the next. On a rough track the metal will form rings inside where one billy rubs against the other.

The best billy is an empty, large or catering size, instant powdered milk tin. My experience is that Sunshine powdered milk tins make the best, although Nescafé tins are also good. Milo and other powdered drinks also come in these large tins. But for whatever reason, Nescafé and powdered milk tins seem to make the best billies. Or, if you are lucky, you might find one similar to the kettle shown on the cover. It was washed ashore on a beach on the Wessel Islands off the coast of Arnhem Land in the Northern Territory.

Always stand the billy on the edge of the fire and on the down-wind side of the flames with the seam facing out. The seam is the most vulnerable part of the tin as it is pressed together. Excessive heat may cause it to split especially just above the waterline. However, treated with care, a good bush billy will last several years.

Never stand a billy on top of the fire as it is likely to fall over as the wood burns down, spilling the contents and perhaps putting the fire out or scalding those sitting close by.

If you place the billy carefully on the fire you can avoid the worst bits and pieces of half-burnt stick and ash falling into it. There's an old trick of floating a piece of stick in the water to attract flying ash and other debris. I've never found this to work very well and you can usually fish out the larger impurities before you make the tea or whatever. The smoke will flavour the water and you should consider this to be an essential and tasty part of the process.

Swiss Army Knife (SAK)

This is an invaluable little item which, while not cheap to buy, is worth its weight in gold. Keep it clean and sharp. I always go for the medium to small varieties with a few gadgets. The larger ones are too big to keep in

Swinging the Billy

An essential skill for all accomplished bush cooks and not as difficult as it seems.

First check the wire handle. If it isn't sound - do not proceed.

Order everyone back.

Hold the top of the wire firmly in your best hand. Swing it forward and then back a metre or so before swinging it in a full circle. Swing it directly over your head at least twice round in a circle. On the second swing pause for a moment at the highest point and utter a loud cry.

Don't pause for too long!

You could practice with cold water first.

To pour a billy

Hold the wire handle a little down from the top of the arch and exert pressure to cause the contents to pour over the point where the wire on the other side joins the rim of the billy.

your pocket without them chafing a hole. Try to get an SAK with a tin opener, corkscrew, screwdriver, an awl, scissors, a small saw and two blades. A toothpick and tweezers are also useful. I used to keep mine attached to me by a cord which meant I didn't lose it every time I crawled under the Toyota. And, if I lent it to anyone, I came with the knife — a threat sure to guarantee its return.

Knife, fork, spoon and tin opener

If you have a good SAK you don't need a tin opener. However a spoon is essential, a fork useful and a knife relieves the pressure on your SAK. Washing them and keeping them clean will always be a problem.

Camp oven

This is obviously not a utensil for the hiker. Camp ovens come in a variety of sizes. A useful one measures about thirty centimetres in diameter and weighs a few kilos. It must be made of cast iron and, unlike the billy, should have a lid. They are available from good camping stores and army surplus supplies stores although there is no evidence that they were ever used by the army! They are easily cleaned with a good rinse and wipe. Remember, don't use harsh abrasives on them. After cleaning your camp oven, and before you put it away, oil it. This stops it rusting. You can heat water in a camp oven and use it as a makeshift washing-up bowl which will also clean the oven at the same time.

You can clean billies, frying pans and any other utensils (but not your camp oven) with fine wood ash which absorbs grease, or sand which works as an abrasive. Sand is hard on enamel and steel surfaces as well as your fingertips. But it does work!

Griller

A camp grill, consisting of two loosely hinged wire frames with handles, is a very useful item. A sliding bracket on the handles fastens the frames together so that meat or bread can be sandwiched between them. The griller can be placed over embers to toast or grill the contents. It is relatively cheap to buy and light to carry. Cleaning is easy — just burn it off after use.

Barbecue plate

Definitely not an item for the lightweight camper! However, some intrepid travellers strap them to the front of their trucks. They need only a light dusting off before throwing on the fire.

The great Australian barbecue is such an institution that no bush cooking book would be complete without reference to this heavy object. Choose a steel plate, preferably with a hole in the middle to allow fat to drain into the fire. Flash versions are dished but you must have one that is at least a quarter of an inch thick. Don't clean it when you are finished. Leave it coated with some fat so it doesn't rust although this is a problem in dusty conditions. Clean it on the fire immediately before cooking by burning it off and dousing with water and then re-oil. A good stiff steel brush is an essential item if you are going to use a barbecue plate.

Frying pan

While it is true that you can cook almost anything in a frying pan I am somewhat ambivalent about them. However, some people won't leave home without one.

A frying pan isn't easy to use on an open fire as the typically plastic handle has a tendency to burn. Try to find one with a long metal handle, but be careful not to burn yourself when you pick it up as the metal will get very hot. A cast-iron version is by far the best, however, you could substitute the camp oven instead. Frying pans are awkward to keep clean because you can't easily heat water in them without slopping it. They have a tendency to attract food that sticks tenaciously to the sides and base. Avoid aluminium versions and non-stick varieties otherwise teflon may soon form a part of your diet.

Shovel

Get a shovel, not a spade, with a long handle. Not only can you use it to get yourself out of a bog but also you can bury, dispatch, retrieve, cook, prop, wedge, slice, move and squash things with it. Remember, a shovel can easily be left behind when you break camp, so create a place specifically for it and make sure that whoever uses it returns it, preferably, to that place when they have finished.

Water

Still the most under-appreciated commodity in the bush, water is a better thirst quencher than anything else. While beer is a close second you really can't drink beer in the heat of the day. Anyway most people won't want to if they have a day's work or travelling ahead of them.

I have drunk green water and brown water. Interestingly enough the only water that ever made me sick was crystal clear. It just goes to show that you cannot judge purity by colour. The main problem with water is that it tastes best when it is cool, not cold, and keeping water cool in the bush is not easy.

Waterbags

Waterbags are made from canvas and come in a variety of sizes, including large versions that you hang on the veranda. Most waterbags, however, flap sadly, dry as a bone, from the bull bars of vehicles. They are useful only to dogs that find the bags at a convenient height for leg cocking when the vehicles are parked in front of the store.

First lesson — place your waterbag high enough so it doesn't get christened by canines!

An old Aboriginal bushman told me once that a shovel was a man's best friend. It would get you out of a bog, you could cook your steak on it, you could use it to bury your rubbish, and when you died it could be used to bury you. Never go bush without a good shovel.

A rough, though not infallible, guide to water purity is the quantity of little critters that can be seen living in it. Water without life is probably not potable. Strain the water to get rid of wildlife that may be best not consumed. Some clean cloth, perhaps a tea towel, can be used for straining. For the fastidious — call in to your local outdoor shop and pick up some water purifying tablets. They will make the water taste of chlorine though.

15

*On one trip when the weather
was particularly hot a
companion told me about the
water in a well we would
soon pass. He stressed that its
purity was matched by no
other and that it was the best
and the sweetest water in the
world. When we arrived at
the well, parched and ready
for a drink, we drank our fill
and replenished the waterbag.
    I agreed that the water
certainly tasted good. As we
drove off splashes of water
from the overfilled waterbag
sprinkled the windscreen and
dried almost at once leaving
sharp white crystals of salt.
    When we stopped later I
noted that the waterbag was
covered with a fur of crystals
rapidly acquiring the deep
hues of the desert dust. Talk
about sweet water indeed!
You could have exported it —
for the minerals alone.*

The second lesson is that a waterbag must be pampered. Some people wonder why a waterbag always seems to leak. Well, they are supposed to leak since it is the evaporation that cools the water inside. When you first buy your waterbag, soak it in cold water for at least twenty-four hours. Then fill it up with water and keep it filled so that it doesn't dry out. An old bush bloke told me that if the bag is first filled with boiling water it lasts much longer. I don't know about this. Since the canvas is always wet it will rot after several months. If your waterbag survives a season, dry it out and store it safely. You may get another season out of it.

The waterbag is a good measure of the quality of the water. Because evaporation in dry climates is rapid, salts form on the outside of the bag if present in any quantity in the water. This also indicates the level of impurities present.

Jerry cans and other containers

The water container is such a basic item it is easy to forget it. Don't. You need to think very carefully about the amount of water you will require. Take plenty in case of emergency. Don't rely on others or tax the hospitality of locals whose supply may be limited for their own essential needs.

You need to allow at least two and a half litres of drinking water a day in cool weather and five litres a day in really hot weather. These quantities do not include water for washing, washing up or cooking. Allow an additional litre an hour for strenuous activities such as walking, working and climbing in hot weather.

Carry water in a stout plastic jerry-can designed for the purpose. Make sure the cap fits well and that it does not leak. And always keep the cap firmly screwed in place when the container is not being used and make sure children understand these simple rules.

Treat these containers with care as they can split. They melt at a fairly low temperature so don't leave them close to the fire. It pays to have both large and small water containers, such as twenty-five litre and ten litre sizes. You can decant water from the larger container into the smaller one for pouring and easier handling.

Always have at least two containers. If one does split you have a reserve supply. Some up-market containers come complete with a small tap and many have provision for one to be fitted. Avoid the tap. Not only is the device vulnerable to knocks which eventually result in cracks and leaks but the taps themselves tend to drip after a short time and so waste your water.

Camp site

In the bush while the universe is your kitchen it is helpful to plan your camp before you start cooking or even making your fire. The most critical factor is the wind, although, if it is hot, the orientation of the sun is also important. Before siting your camp think carefully about shade. You will need shade for cooking, eating and relaxing during the early evening and you may also need shade in the early morning if it is really hot.

Place preparation areas, vehicles and sleeping areas upwind so that you don't spend your time sitting in the smoke. More importantly, if the fire should get away you won't see your life investment go up in smoke as well. Remember that even small, controlled cooking fires can release sparks and that petrol is very flammable. Always remove any dry grass caught under your vehicle. It could quickly spell disaster if a spark ignites it.

Try to keep utensils and food off the ground. Set aside a place where food can be placed after it is cooked. I've seen many a tasty meal ruined because sand was inadvertently scuffed onto it — marauding children are often the culprits. The tragedy would have been avoided if the pan had been placed on a table, stump or drum.

Fire

Your campfire is the centre of the cooking activity. Its heat and size, and your ability to control it, will determine your success or failure. Many campers in the bush assume that all you need do is heap up some old sticks, and the more the better, set a match to them and you can cook everything you need. While it's true that some recipes require a very large fire, most don't.

Don't let children or adults use water containers as seats in your vehicle or in the camp. On one occasion a rather fat little boy sat on a water container in the back of my truck and went through it. Not only did he get a very wet bum but I lost twenty-five litres of valuable water.

Remember
You can't cook many things without water – but, more importantly, without water, you die.

A large fire does not necessarily mean that it will be hot enough for cooking either and if the conflagration is so large that you can't get near it, then you can't cook dinner in any case. Care must be taken to ensure the fire is controlled and you must make yourself familiar with any local fire regulations. Be very careful if it is windy and dry and if there is a lot of undergrowth, dry grass or other scrub. If you start a bushfire you endanger both your own life and the lives of other people, quite apart from the damage that you cause to the local environment and beyond.

Choose an open clear area, with at least a three metre clearance on all sides. A dry, sandy creek bed is ideal. Once again, note the direction of the wind before you do anything. Keep the fire small and feed dry sticks into it from the leeward side. For most cooking a hot ember fire, with little flame and usually little smoke, is preferable.

Light the fire at least half an hour before you want to start cooking so that a good ember bed is ready when you are. You can then develop heat of different intensity over different areas for different tasks. Have plenty of dry wood handy to feed and maintain the fire. Try to appreciate which wood is best for the fire. Indigenous people have an intimate knowledge,

It's easy to get lost in the bush. If you must go off alone, don't go without a compass, a box of matches and plenty of water and an agreed contingency plan. Reflected sunlight from a small mirror can be seen many kilometres away and could save your life and it is a better solution than setting fire to the bush!

Aboriginal people traditionally used low windbreaks and small fires to keep warm in the cold desert nights. Sleeping in this manner, with a small fire between each person, it is surprising how warm you can keep even with minimal covering. Wood is carefully selected to ensure maximum heat and burn time. Small sleeping depressions (lau in Pitjantjatjara) hollowed to accommodate the shape of your body, make sleeping on the sand more comfortable.

A Jigalong man making camp in the Gibson Desert, Western Australia, 1976.

18

Fire is very important for Aboriginal people and is used as an effective tool to help manage the environment. It was also used as a means of communication, since smoke from fires could be seen kilometres away, signalling the presence of kin or strangers.

A man I knew once unsuccessfully chased a willy-willy in a Toyota in the mistaken belief that it was a column of smoke put up by me. The willy-willy, forming over burnt-out country, consisted of charcoal and burnt debris, so it did look more like smoke than dust. This seemingly strange behaviour was occasioned by our becoming separated during a survey in open country in the Hamersley ranges of Western Australia. I had told him that in the event that he lost me, I would put up a smoke.

On a distant hillside with the aid of my binoculars I watched with increasing dismay as I saw my transport and supplies receding ever further away from where I was. Finally, I fired the hillside and as the willy-willy dissipated and my friend realised his error, he looked back and saw my smoke, and I am relieved to say he turned around and hurriedly drove back to find me.

passed from generation to generation, of the different types and properties of wood. Over time the bush camper will begin to gain similar knowledge.

As a general guide, solid, heavy wood burns hotter and slower than lighter, less solid wood. River gum burns quicker than mulga (*acacia*). Desert oak burns slowly. Don't be tempted to break off green wood. It won't burn and it damages the tree.

If the wood is wet, as sometimes happens, use bark, particularly stringy and paperbark, to start the fire. Bark can be collected from the trunks of trees and dead twigs can be removed from trees. These dry out quicker in the air and make good kindling if protected from the rain.

Once you get the fire started, collect dead wood and stack it close enough to the fire to allow it to dry out but not catch. Place some under cover for later use. A wet smoky fire is an abomination and makes cooking very difficult. Tropical Australia in the wet season provides the worst conditions, in my experience, and such circumstances require patience, ingenuity and perseverance.

Some people place a ring of stones round the fire so it looks attractive, a bit like a McCubbin painting. Apart from some unwarranted preoccupation with tidiness, I have never been able to see the utility of this. Moreover, if the rocks have been subject to any moisture, they may actually explode when they become hot. Flying fragments of stone will make short work of the camp cook before the diners get a chance to do likewise. In any event avoid making your fire on rocky ground if possible.

Once, after several days of searing heat in the heart of the Great Victoria Desert I was camping with a small group of Pitjantjatjara people. We had been working hard in extremely hot conditions in heavy sand dune country. After dark, and as a special treat (it was my birthday), I opened a tin of satsuma plums I had been hoarding — a rare and unique commodity in those circumstances. Someone shouted, 'Cool change coming' and, as I turned, I became aware of a low, distant roar to the south west. The roar grew, drawing closer and getting louder by the minute. I wondered what it was.

People started to run about in the dark, securing swags, dampening fires and heading for cover. When the wind hit it did so with a force and impact that was unimaginable. Fires were blown out; plates and mugs were thrown across the campsite; blankets, tarps and buckets were thrown about and strewn everywhere. Like my colleagues I got down behind a fallen tree and hoped I wouldn't be decapitated by flying debris.

When the storm abated — it had lasted only five minutes but seemed endless — I set about recovering my possessions and disinterring my swag. Then I remembered my plums. Amazingly, they were more or less where I'd left them, the opened tin still upright. I soon discovered the reason why they hadn't blown over. The tin was full of sand. Happy birthday - at least the weather was cooler.

Several of the recipes require cooking directly on the coals. This was the method preferred traditionally by Indigenous Australians. It still has many advantages. It requires no utensils. Fat drains into the fire so the meat is not swimming in polyunsaturated stuff that is bad for you, and the fire itself imparts a unique flavour to the food.

For those who like their meat rare this process tends to cook the outside quickly leaving the vital juices and the meat red in the centre. A disadvantage is that it is difficult to make an ember fire that has no ash which, of course, will stick to the food. It is also difficult to make a fire that has no dust and grit which also sticks to food and which makes mastication unpleasant and your dentist delighted to see you.

The secret is to make a hot fire with medium-sized twigs and branches that will form solid glowing coals, with little or no ash. Make sure it is well above the ground to avoid the sand or grit upon which the fire is built. Obviously, heavy dense wood makes better fuel for this process than light quick-burning varieties. Success, therefore, may depend on your having or acquiring a degree of local knowledge.

Wind

Wind is the main culprit when it comes to dust and grit. The bush is a windy place and there is never any shortage of dust, and desert sandstorms can be quite dramatic.

Note the direction of the wind. Become familiar with likely shifts during the night. Use natural cover or any of your gear and apparatus to create a windbreak. Your vehicle makes a good windbreak. Block the underside with boxes or gear to prevent the draught blowing under the car. Keep down behind it with a small hot fire in the lee of the shelter.

It's best to be ready for storms, willy-willies and the like. But, even in a mere moderate wind there's plenty of dust about. Try to keep food that you are not preparing, or about to eat, covered or stored in covered containers. Keep tops on water containers, pots and pans, to minimise the chances of dust and grit becoming an unwelcome accompaniment to your dinner.

I gave up sleeping on a camp stretcher years ago because it was too cold. One memorable night I woke about 1.00 am and realised I was being air-cooled from beneath. There was a heavy frost and I was exposed to wind chill as well. You certainly learn the hard way!

People often suffer unnecessarily from the cold during the central Australian winter because they fail to appreciate the effect of wind and cold air. Sitting up at a table is probably the coldest place imaginable in such circumstances.

Indigenous people select their camp to avoid the force of the wind and they create windbreaks behind which they sit or lie.

Sleeping on the ground on a thin but adequate mattress is in fact much more comfortable and much warmer than a camp stretcher. In any case, spring loaded, camp stretchers are notorious finger breakers as you struggle to put them up. Leaving the stretcher at home means one less item of clobber to cart around.

And don't be misled into thinking that being off the ground will protect you from snakes. They can find refuge under the cot and you might step on one when you get up! If you camp on the ground, however, don't leave your swag unrolled. Snakes like swags, especially if they're still warm. Avoid these unwelcome guests. Pack up your swag and place it in a tree or on the back of your truck.

Protection of the natural environment

Indigenous Australians had their own ways of ensuring that they did not over-exploit the natural environment. This allowed them to occupy and utilise the continental landmass and off-shore islands and reefs for many thousands of years. They developed a sustainable economy based upon the environment that they relied on for sustenance. To some extent, and with the possible exception of fire, the technology they employed ensured that over-exploitation was not likely.

This changed with the arrival of the white man. His firearms and other technologies altered fundamentally the Australian environment in a relatively short space of time. The demise of indigenous species is one of the regrettable hallmarks of white settlement in this country over the last two hundred years. Australian law now protects many native animals and plant species in an attempt to stem their destruction and demise.

Many Aboriginal and Torres Strait Islander peoples have retained their rights to hunt and forage over many parts of the continent and to take, for personal consumption, animals and plants which are otherwise protected. Some are fighting to have these rights recognised through the establishment of native title rights. However, these rights cannot be extended to the broader Australian population without seriously jeopardising the integrity of the fauna and flora that remain.

Nectar from the Grevillea can be used to make a sweet drink.

The Indigenous recipes described here are still used by Aboriginal and Torres Strait Islander peoples in the course of normal living. The recipes and the taking of the wild life involved are the business of Indigenous Australians and cannot be emulated by other bush travellers. This is not to say that they have no relevance to the broader non-Indigenous Australian public.

Non-indigenous ingredients can be substituted for the indigenous items identified in the recipe, for example, a sheep can be substituted for a kangaroo; but check with the farmer first! A piglet could be substituted for a wombat. Order a fresh farmyard turkey and cook it in the manner described for the Australian bush turkey. Rabbit is another suitable alternative for several of the recipes.

More importantly an appreciation of Indigenous cooking and cooking methods adds to the general appreciation of the first and original settlers of this continent. Non-Indigenous people are now more aware of the enduring and rich cultural heritage Indigenous Australians contribute to the bush, the country and the nation.

And other things...

The list is endless but it is surprising how little you actually need. Don't forget that you will need a box or two of matches. A bucket is very useful and it may be needed for collecting water in any case. A good galvanised one can be used to heat water although this doesn't do the galvanising much good. A plastic bucket is useful for mixing flour.

A small folding table makes cooking preparation a whole lot easier and chairs generally make eating more comfortable. A gas lamp is helpful but it attracts moths and the mantles and glass are both easily broken. They may be more trouble than they are worth.

A good torch, however, is essential. The rechargeable types have improved in the last few years and can be recharged from a vehicle cigarette lighter.

A steel trunk is useful for storage especially on the ground.

Finally, a roll of masking tape, some rope and a piece of wire are always useful for a range of purposes too numerous to mention here.

With the above you have the *essential* items for bush cooking. But remember you could manage without any, except your Swiss Army Knife, of course, if you had to.

recipes

Indigenous bush recipes

Some of the ingredients used in the following recipes are protected species and can be hunted and gathered only by Indigenous Australians. Non-Indigenous people should make appropriate substitutions.

Drinks

Traditional Indigenous peoples made a variety of drinks. Generally though water was the staple drink. The First Australians readily adopted tea and coffee which were introduced by the first European settlers. Sugar, also introduced by the Europeans, was more convenient and more readily available than traditional equivalents like honey and nectar.

Indigenous people have developed their own distinctive methods of making tea. A recipe for a more conventional tea is given under Drinks in the Non-Indigenous recipes section.

Billy tea (Indigenous method 1)

Take a large billy and fill it about two-thirds full with water. Heat on the fire until the water is warm. Throw in two or three handfuls of tea and leave it to heat until the water boils. Take the billy off the fire and stand it to one side.

Fill a second billy with a litre of water. From a height of about half a metre pour the cold water into the hot tea. Add as much sugar as required to the mixture, usually about 500 grams to two to three litres. Pour back and forth from one billy to the other, allowing a good distance between the two containers.

Drink, diluted with cold water to taste.

Maralinga Lands, South Australia, 1988

Billy tea (Indigenous method 2)

Take a large, approximately 2.5-litre capacity, billy and fill it two-thirds full with water and place on a hot fire. Add a small handful of tea leaves. Bring to the boil. Remove from the fire.

Fill a second billy about one-third full and from this billy add cold water to the tea billy and fill up to the top. Add two large handfuls of white sugar and then pour back into the first billy and then pour half back into the second, so that both are half full.

Then fill a third billy with cold water and add this to the other two billies. Then pour back and forth between the billies until tea, water and sugar are properly mixed and the three billies contain equal quantities of tea. Serve to the tea drinkers.

Desert south of Balgo, Western Australia, 1980

Sweet sugar lerp

Some eucalypts are host to psyllids, small insects whose young secrete a white, waxy, sweet substance called lerp which can be eaten raw or mixed with water to form a sweet drink. Trees infected by the insect are often covered with the white secretion which is similar to crystallised sugar. It is collected from the leaves by shaking and brushing so the lerp falls into a container. It may also be collected from the ground beneath the tree where it may fall in large quantities. It can be dissolved in a little water to form a light syrup and drunk or eaten raw like a sweet or lolly.

Maralinga Lands, South Australia, 1988

Sweet nectar

A number of plants have nectar rich flowers. In particular, desert grevillea can have nectar-bearing flowers in a good season, particularly after rain, that literally drip with honey. The flowers can be shaken in water and the resultant sweet drink consumed directly from the bowl or dish, or sucked from sponge-like wads of grass that have been immersed in the liquid.

Sandy Desert, Western Australia, 1975

Breads

Damper, the staple bread style food in outback Australia, is often served to tourists in expensive restaurants. To retain the authentic taste, however, it must be cooked in an open fire. Aboriginal people traditionally made damper from the ground seeds of certain grasses and shrubs. This involved intensive preparation both in collecting the seeds in the first place, and grinding them. The introduction of European flour revolutionised damper production. However, damper has probably been a staple in the Indigenous Australian diet for tens of thousands of years.

Damper

Take approximately two and a half to three kilos of white flour. Empty onto a flourbag or piece of cardboard or into a large bowl if one is available. A small handful of baking powder may also be added. Mix well. Add sufficient water to form a dough having the consistency of plasticine. Dust the bowl or flourbag with flour to prevent it from sticking. Knead it well for at least ten minutes. The mixture is about right when it does not stick to the hands or bowl and has a smooth creamy consistency. Set to one side.

The first damper I cooked came out with the consistency of yellow candle wax because I had made the mixture too wet.

Creating the perfect damper is a matter of practice. It should turn out light and full of air holes: a sign that it has been properly kneaded. The outside crust should be free of cracks which tend to trap ash and sand.

Prepare a hot fire in readiness. When it has burnt down, clear away the hot coals with a stick, leaving a clean hot bed of sand and ash. Sprinkle the cooking area with flour and then lay the dough down onto the hot sand and ash and press it out flat. Draw a layer of hot sand and ash back over the top of the damper with a stick. The hot sand acts as insulation and prevents the damper from being burned by direct contact with coals. After about twenty minutes, lift the damper and turn it over in the ashes.

Tap the damper to test if it is cooked. It should produce a hollow thudding sound. Take it from the fire and remove any excess ash by lightly beating the damper or brushing it with leaves.

Maralinga Lands, South Australia, 1988

For the finicky, damper can be cooked in a camp oven. Follow the same steps, including turning the damper over when it is part cooked. Make sure that the camp oven is not too hot. It must be covered with hot sand and ashes *before* burning coals are placed over it. Use a shovel to distribute the hot sand and coals for the best results.

A good damper has few cracks in it and should not be burnt. Eat it fresh, since even a great damper becomes hard and unpalatable after only several hours.

Fat fella tucker

These are called Johnny cakes in some areas.

Make up a dough mixture of flour, water and baking powder. Knead it into small cakes. Place enough cooking oil, beef dripping or lard, in a frying pan or suitable container to deep fry the cakes. Heat until smoking. Place the cakes in the fat and cook for about five minutes or until golden brown.

Eat hot with cocky's joy (treacle), jam or your favoured spread.

I do not recommend these for people with a heart condition or of weak constitution.

Maralinga Lands, South Australia, 1988

Pancakes

Make a runny mixture of flour and water, adding an egg or two to taste, if you've got any. Beat the mixture well. It should have the consistency of raw cream. Traditionally the mixture should stand for several hours before use, although this may not be practical. Heat an oiled pan in a hot fire and pour enough of the mixture into the pan to make a small pancake. You can add currants or sultanas if you like. When it's cooked on one side, flip it over and cook the other side. Serve with lemon, sugar, treacle or jam.

Maralinga Lands, South Australia, 1988

Bush twist

Make a dough mixture, as described above for damper. Knead it into a long sausage about one centimetre thick and up to twenty-five centimetres long. Take a slim green stick and wind the dough in a serpentine fashion down its length. Cook over hot coals, making sure the stick does not catch alight. This requires some skill as the dough can cook too fast and burn or remain raw in parts.

Maralinga Lands, South Australia, 1988

Meat

The kangaroo has a particularly important place in the lives of many Aboriginal people. The animal has strong spiritual associations with the Dreaming and is also a highly prized food item. The meat of the red kangaroo (*Macropus rufus*) is particularly popular. However, there are many different types of kangaroo across Australia and, in some areas, the smaller wallabies are favoured as having especially succulent and soft meat. The recipe provided here was collected from the southern Pitjantjatjara people on the Maralinga Lands in South Australia.

Kumana Queama ready for the drive back to camp with some red kangaroos: Yalata, South Australia, 1981.

Kangaroo

This not a recipe for most Australians as some species of kangaroo are protected by law. For the Pitjantjatjara and indeed for many other desert peoples, the cookbook instructions read something like this:

I remember eating a kangaroo tail with a lawyer for the Aboriginal Legal Service in Western Australia. It was a meal that formed part of a ritual cycle but was informal enough for all that. We were presented with the tail of a kangaroo, just cooked, in both senses of the word. However, there was some concern among the men that the lawyer had to sit on the ground like the rest of us. Eventually, an old chair, without a back, was produced and presented to the lawyer which he duly sat on.

Sensing an injustice, and being heartily sick of sitting in the dirt, I asked where my chair was. I was told that anthropologists always sit on the ground and that was their place. Lawyers, on the other hand, had to be mollycoddled and should always be given a chair to sit on. I noted, with some satisfaction however, that he made less headway with the kangaroo tail than I did.

Take a recently hunted kangaroo. Gut the animal within an hour or two of death, laying it on its back with its hind legs splayed out. Dislocate the legs at the thigh and push them outwards, revealing the stomach clear of the legs. Place bushes on one side of the carcass and make a short incision in the lower stomach. Pull the intestines out onto the bushes. Detach the lower intestine approximately fifty centimetres from the rectum and expel pellets. Open the stomach and empty and clean the tripe. Discard all but the lower intestine.

Sharpen a short peeled stick at both ends. Leaving the stomach outside the carcass and lying on the leaves insert the stick into the sides of the stomach incision to form a suture, which stitches the cut together. Wrap the piece of lower intestine four or five times around the stick, in a figure of eight, to tie up the stick and stomach incision. The end is then impaled on one end of the sharpened stick. There is a traditional prohibition that forbids the washing of the blood of the red kangaroo from hands or implements.

Ground oven cooking must be done in sand or at least sandy soil. Dig a small pit approximately one and a half metres long and forty centimetres deep. Heap a large quantity of dry wood into the pit to a height of about one metre. When the fire is burning well, place the carcass, with

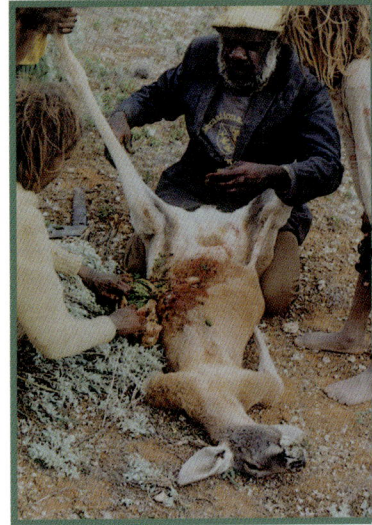

Kumana Queama and members of his family gutting kangaroos: Yalata, South Australia, 1981.

Removing lower intestine to tie up suture in belly after stomach removed.

stomach detached, on top of the conflagration and, using the tail or legs, turn it over several times until all the fur is singed off. Place the carcass to one side until the fire has burnt down to a hot bed of ashes. Cut off the tail.

Bury the carcass in the ashes with legs uppermost and shovel hot sand on its stomach. Lay the tail alongside it. Pile sand and then ashes over it so the rear legs and front paws protrude a little from the pit. Cook for approximately one hour.

The tail is traditionally the best meat and can also be skinned and boiled up in a camp oven with a few vegetables. The cartilage is sticky

An elderly man taught me how to tie up a kangaroo in order to carry it back to the camp. This technique predated the use of vehicles. Carrying a kangaroo on your head must have been a challenging task since a typical animal can weigh up to 50 kilos.

All directions are given in relation to the dead animal lying on its back, head uppermost, with the person by the kangaroo's tail. The kangaroo must first be gutted and sutured, as described above, and a portion of the gut retained for tying up.

Take the hind-leg on the left and tie it to the tail, using the intestine which has been rubbed in sand. Take the left forearm and bring back between the rear left leg and tail. The right forearm is brought outside of the rear right leg so that the leg is pushed forward towards the head and held close to the body. Tie the right forearm to the rear left leg and knot along with the left forearm tight against the tail.

Jack May with a kangaroo tied up and carried in the traditional manner: bush camp north of Yalata, South Australia, 1981.

The tied-up kangaroo is lifted by its tail and forearms, with the head hanging down to the side and balanced on the hunter's head. If the stomach suture breaks, the blood spills out and this is regarded as a disgrace. Tying the kangaroo up the wrong way was regarded as a punishable offence. If a man carried a kangaroo the wrong way, for example, across the shoulders, he was subject to ridicule. People might say, for example, that he thought he was carrying a rabbit.

Yalata, South Australia, 1981

33

to the touch and the meat rather elusive but the overall taste is excellent. The tail cooked in the ashes, as described above, is a more challenging proposition.

Pull the whole carcass out of the pit and beat off surplus ash with leafy branches. Butcher the carcass with an axe, dividing the head, back, ribs, forelegs, hind-legs and tail. The liver, heart, kidneys and other internal organs are also removed, although they may be taken out earlier and cooked in the ashes of a separate fire if preferred. The lungs are cooked inside with the ribs and can be eaten or they can be given to the dogs.

Once, in the Kimberley region, I spent several days visiting Aboriginal communities with a lawyer from Perth. (Not the same one as sat on the chair.) He was not altogether comfortable in the bush while I had the advantage of knowing my way around a bit.

On a cattle station, owned and run by an Aboriginal community, we were invited to have tea with an old white fellow who had lived in the bush most of his life. Just what he was doing living on that particular station, I can't recall, but he was one of the most hospitable men I can remember.

His home was a converted tin shed and his oven an old wood stove. Being a cattle station, there was no shortage of beef. He did us a roast.

He delicately cut the joint into one centimetre slabs and piled four or five onto each plate. Then followed a heap of potato and pumpkin with some gravy. The meat alone was enough to feed a small platoon for several days.

My legal colleague, whose usual cuisine was obviously both more delicate and moderate than that which was set before him (I suspect he was a closet vegetarian) blanched at the pile of food and the wedges of dark red meat. Fearing to offend he valiantly attempted to eat what was set before him. He failed quite spectacularly.

It's interesting how those who live in the bush and whose heart and mind occupy the vast open spaces and remote, unsophisticated dwelling places have a way of getting equal with lawyers and city folk.

I ate all of mine and remembered sitting on the ground while the lawyer sat on the chair.

Bush turkey (*Ardeotis australis*)

Bush turkeys are a protected species and cannot be shot or taken.

The poor old turkey is a heavy bird. To fly they take off into the wind like a plane. But they are so slow taking off that they prefer to skulk away between the spinifex rather than risk airborne flight and this makes them easy prey.

The early white settlers exploited these birds with the result that they became extinct over many areas of the continent. A flock of turkeys is a rare sight, although they are sometimes seen in pairs or singly on northern plains. If you have the good fortune to see one remember that until recently they were more numerous than they are today and were an important food item for Indigenous peoples.

Turkey was very popular with Aboriginal people because of the rich flavour of its light-brown meat.

Pluck the turkey and remove the lower organs by means of a small cut in the lower abdomen. Singe the plucked body on a hot fire. Prepare a small pit and build a good fire over it. When the fire has burnt down clear away the burning coals. Place the turkey on its front in the pit, cover with hot sand, ash and finally coals. Cooking time should be about forty-five minutes.

A variation of the traditional method of cooking is to line the pit with sheets of tin or corrugated iron. One old man did this for me on the plains behind Eighty Mile Beach in Western Australia. The turkey is placed on the tin and another piece of iron laid on top. Hot sand and coals are then heaped onto the tin to form a complete earth oven. The bird was cooked for over an hour and was taken out well cooked in its own juices and steam.

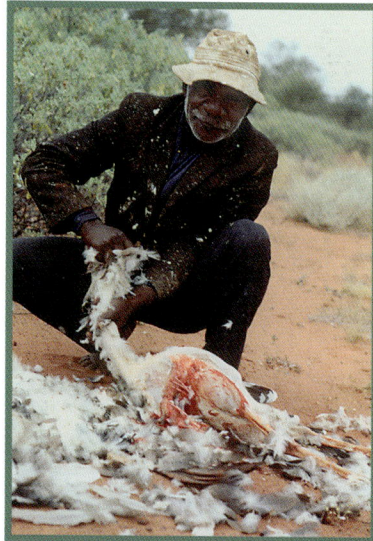

Plucking a bush turkey.

Once, on the huge plains of the inland Pilbara, Western Australia, I was visiting a remote station, home to a ranger who had care of a huge property that was formerly an agricultural research centre. I was accompanying a group of Aboriginal men with whom I was working. As we came over a low rise we saw a small flock of six bush turkeys. One was promptly dispatched by one of the men using a .22 rifle from the back of the truck. He jumped down and recovered the bird.

Realising that they were about to visit a ranger with a known interest in the local wildlife they stuffed the carcass into a tool box and hoped the feathers wouldn't poke out off the poorly fitting lid.

At the Ranger's residence and while the men were discussing the season, the location of cattle and which waterholes were nearly dry, I noticed a diary on a side table, listing sightings of wild life on the surrounding plains. My host saw my interest and suggested I have a closer look. It fell open at a recent annotation recording a flock of six *Ardeotis australis* on the plain south west of the homestead. If I'd had a pencil handy I 'd have changed the six to a five.

The men enjoyed their dinner that night.

Emu (*Dromaius novae-hollandiae*)

Traditionally emu was a much-prized food. Although often fatty the meat was tender and made a welcome change from kangaroo.

Like turkey, emus are protected and should not be shot. The traditional Pitjantjatjara cookbook might read something like this:

Take a recently speared emu and pluck it. Remove the intestines via a small cut in the abdomen. Stuff this hole with feathers to keep the insides clean. Cook the emu, covered with hot sand and ashes, in an earth oven for about one hour. When cooked, remove from the fire and joint it. Distribute the meat and eat.

Maralinga Lands, South Australia, 1981

Emu (foreground) ready for cooking when the fire has burned down: Great Victoria Desert, Western Australia.

Echidna or porcupine (spiny anteater) (*Tachyglossus aculeatus*)

Once again, this is not a recipe for non-Indigenous Australians.

According to the Pitjantjatjara of the Maralinga Lands the desert echidna lives in a hole in the sand. It never comes out at night if there is a full moon, because, it is said, it thinks the moon is a devil or *mamu*. Pitjantjatjara people gave me the details set out below. The traditional cooking instructions would be something like:

> Track an echidna (known as *tjilka marta* in Pitjantjatjara) in the desert sand. Only an expert can tell from the tracks which way the animal is going. Dig the animal out and dispatch it with a sharp blow with the shovel.

Traditionally, Aboriginal people living in desert regions did not have access to salt. Some communities still retain a prohibition on putting salt on bush meat. It can be added to meat like beef, lamb and rabbit and to other western foods.

37

Remove the lower intestines and stomach by means of a small cut in the belly. Any fat should be replaced in the abdominal cavity and the cut sutured with a small stick (*tipinpa*) and dry sand sprinkled on the cut to seal it. In a hot fire, singe the carcass to remove most of the spines, the remainder of which can then be dislodged with an axe. When the fire has died down clear an area in the embers and lay the echidna in the ashes. Cover with hot sand and then ashes and cook for about half an hour.

The echidna is very fatty and rich. The flesh is whitish with a mild and pleasant taste. The skin and remaining bristles are a little like pork crackling but with a rather bitter after-taste.

Great Victoria Desert, South Australia, 1982

Once, while out hunting wombat on the Nullarbor, we finally stopped for a late lunch. I was starving. As the honoured guest, I was offered the liver, still warm, from the carcass of a newly butchered wombat. 'It's the best part', my friends told me enthusiastically. They told me to cook it on the embers of a small fire we'd prepared.

Initially, my hunger was such that I thought it tasted like paté. The liver, however, was large (only a little smaller than a sheep's liver) and, as I got to the still-raw middle, the taste began to inform all my senses with nausea. I don't remember how I finished the meal — but I didn't join the clean-plate club.

Echidna ready for cooking.

Wombat (*Lasiorhinus latifrons*)

At Yalata in South Australia, wombat is a favourite meat. It also is a protected species so it is not a meat for most Australians. It is cooked in much the same way as kangaroo, feet up in a pit.

Feral cat (*Felix domestica*)

In deference to cat lovers, especially my wife and our two cats, Malcolm and Myrtle, there is no recipe for wild cat (*putjikata*: pussy cat), but it is eaten in desert areas of Australia. I tried to eat one only once, in the Great Sandy Desert. It was so tough that any taste was lost on me. Like most other meat dishes it is gutted and cooked in an earth oven.

Galah (*Cacatua roseicapilla*) (method 1)

The galah is a much-maligned bird, being synonymous in the Australian imagination with stupidity. How it earned this reputation is unclear to me, although I do admit that it has a tendency to throw itself in front of your vehicle on bush roads. Whatever its cerebral capacity it is a great Australian bird. If you wish to try the following recipe, substitute a quail or other small bird from the butcher.

> Kill a galah with a throwing stick. Remove the lower gut through a small cut in the abdomen. Singe all the feathers and then bake in the ashes until cooked. Reputed to be very tough.
>
> *Maralinga Lands, South Australia, 1988*

Galah (*Cacatua roseicapilla*) (method 2)

> Take a dead galah, pluck it, gut it and put it in a billy of water. Place the billy on the fire and bring to the boil. Add a small clean stone or an old boot. Cook for 6–7 hours. Discard the galah and eat the stone or the boot.
>
> *Traditional Australian bush recipe*

Parrot (*Squacus ubiquitus*)

> Procure a dead parrot (originally a chicken), pluck and gut it and place it in a camp oven. Take one bottle of fine brandy and half a bottle of dry vermouth and mix with orange juice. Pour over the bird and cook in the camp oven at a low heat for several hours depending on size and age of parrot. Remove from the fire, discard the parrot and drink the gravy.
>
> *Major Richard Viant, British Army*

After a particularly good season in the desert area around Maralinga, South Australia, the budgerigars reached almost plague proportions. They settled on any shiny surface, including the Toyota roof, in the mistaken belief that it was water. They woke me up on several mornings when I was staying in transportable accommodation at the old atomic test site, sounding just like rain on the roof as literally thousands of birds settled and resettled, disturbed by any slight noise. While many birds would perish, their appearance at this time demonstrated the richness of the desert, however briefly, after good rains.

Once, when driving across the Yule flood plain, in the north west of Western Australia, I ran into a flock of budgerigars that swooped at the wrong moment into the path of my Landrover. It was an expensive mistake for the birds a s I counted nearly forty of them dead on the track. I buried them. When I arrived at my destination and told my story to the leader of the Aboriginal community he was aghast at the waste and told me I should have brought them along with me as they had the makings of a great meal.

40

Budgerigar (Melopsittacus undulatus)

One of the most amazing sights on the plains of the northern Pilbara, Western Australia, is the flocks of budgerigars that swoop and swirl in perfect coordination across the open countryside.

Budgies can be knocked over with a thrown boomerang, if you're good, then plucked and lightly roasted in the ashes. You do need quite a few for a good feed.

Fish, reptiles and other meat

Stingray

On Groote Eylandt, and indeed in many other coastal areas of Arnhem Land, stingray is considered an excellent meal. They are speared in shallow water usually at low tide. The common ray, generally approximately thirty-five centimetres across its wings and a dark-brown or blackish colour, is preferred. The spotted ray is considered inedible. The ray is known as *yimatuwaya* on Groote Eylandt.

The rays have a dangerous barb under the tail that should be treated with extreme caution. Ensure the ray is dead before holding the tail up and knocking the barb backward with a single blow from a stout stick or club. Make sure that the barb is disposed of properly. Don't leave it lying about where someone can tread on it as it is poisonous and will cause a nasty wound.

Cleaning stingray meat with seawater: Wessel Islands, Northern Territory.

Stingray fish balls

Make a small incision in the lower abdomen with your fingernail or a sharp piece of bailer shell. Remove the intestines but retain the liver, placing it to one side. Throw the ray onto a hot fire and leave until cooked through.

Scrape the flesh from the wings, back and tail and place on a rock or a piece of cardboard or a plate if you have one. Pour sea water over the meat to remove the worst of the sand and grit. Squeeze the flesh into fist-sized balls and compress to remove water.

Making stingray meat into balls: Wessel Islands, Northern Territory.

Lay the liver between two layers of eucalyptus leaves and cook it in the ashes. When it is cooked divide the liver between the balls and knead it into them. Make sure they are well mixed. Serve and enjoy.

Galiwink'u, (Elcho Island), Arnhem Land, 1983

On Groote Eylandt the liver was left out of the fish ball but I was told that it could be included if preferred. I also noted that the ray was washed in the sea *after* cooking, as well, to help eliminate the sand.

One afternoon I accompanied a man, armed with a club and a spear who speared seven rays in an hour and a half.

Black-lipped oysters

These oysters are best gathered, and eaten raw, from the rocks in northern Australia as the tide recedes. These have to be one of the treats available to any visitor to the littoral bush. You can also cook them on a slow fire. As usual embers are best. The oysters will open of their own accord when ready to eat.

Wessel Islands, Northern Territory, 1983

Freshwater mussels

Locate the mussels in the mud of a billabong by probing the mud with your toes. Collect enough for a meal. Wash off the worst of the mud from the shells. Prepare a small fire and place the mussels in the ashes taking care that the hinge is downwards. Heat for a few minutes only. The bivalve should open and the contents simmer. Remove from the fire and eat straightaway or when cooled a little.

Amanbidji, Northern Territory, 1983

Freshwater mussels: Amanbidji Station, Northern Territory.

Witchetty grubs (*Xyleutes leucomochla*)

Witchetty grubs are perhaps the most highly prized delicacy of all the bush foods eaten by desert people. Women traditionally collect them but men and boys also participate in this popular social activity.

The grubs are the larvae of the goat moth (*Cossidae*) and are to be found in the roots of *Acacia kempeana*, as well as in other acacias such as *Acacia murrayana*, *Acacia victoriae* and *Acacia ligulata*. The discarded skins of hatched grubs around the base of the plants indicate their presence. The roots are located with a crowbar, traditionally a digging stick, and dug up. The grubs will be found within the root at a slight swelling. Small twigs can be used to prise the grubs out.

42

In more northern desert areas the grubs are found in the outer trunks of eucalyptus trees (unidentified species) growing close to claypans. Their presence is indicated by a bore hole in the trunk. They are extracted by pushing a hooked stick (made in the same way as the pot-lifter described on page 54) into the hole till the grub is encountered and impaled on the hook. Pull it out.

Maku or witchetty grub.

Prepare a hot sand bed close to the fire on which embers have been burning. Clear it of all debris and lay the grubs on the sand. Cover with hot sand and then hot ash and glowing embers. Take care to ensure that the live coals do not come into contact with the grubs. Leave for a few minutes depending on the heat of the sand. Uncover the grubs, turn them over and repeat. Remove from the fire and dust off. Eat.

Maralinga Lands, South Australia, 1988

You may prefer not to eat the head which can be a little crunchy. For a delicious alternative, lightly fry the grubs in oil or fat, with salt, garlic and pepper to taste. Eat hot.

Desert frogs (Notoden nichollsi Parker)

Frogs are a protected species and should be left in peace.

A species of small frog can be found deep down in the sand dunes in areas of Central Australia. Aboriginal women are able to locate the frogs by identifying a low mound of sand, no more than a few centimetres across, on the crest of a dune. It takes a sharp eye and much practice to see this feature which covers the burrow, presumably created by the mother frog when laying her brood. I certainly was never able to see it. There is still much to learn about the behaviour of these amphibians.

The frogs are about five centimetres long, and round and fat like a small puffy ball. They are dark-green or khaki on their back, with black spots, and covered with a thick slime that sticks to the sand. When bruised the

I was on a bush trip once out from Balgo, Western Australia and the Aboriginal women I was with spotted evidence of a nest of these frogs.

A woman rapidly dug a hole down to a depth of about two metres using a billy can. She dug down so deep you couldn't see her above the sand. When she located the nest she began throwing the frogs up to the other women waiting on the edge. As each frog was thrown up out of the hole the women who were catching them sprinkled each one with sand to stop it slipping out of their fingers. They then pressed the frogs' heads back into their bodies by pushing them in with their thumbs while holding the frogs in the palms of their hands, with their fingers grasping the rear of the amphibian. While the excavation continued they kept the frogs cool by covering them with damp sand.

The frog is surprisingly fatty in the rear part but rather bony. However, the whole animal is eaten. I gained special dispensation not to eat the head which I had found to be a quite challenging experience!

frogs excrete a white latex-looking substance. They are found in a nest at a depth of one to two metres or so within a dune where the sand becomes damp. There may be as many as a hundred in each hole.

Frog

Prepare a hot fire. When it has burnt down to good embers clear coals from an area of hot sand and level it . Place two or three frogs at a time on the hot sand and cover with additional hot sand. Cover the sand with embers. Leave for a few minutes. Uncover, turn the frogs, and cover again. After some five minutes or less of cooking, serve the frogs, having first removed intestinal contents from the anal vent by running your thumb down the lower belly. Eat the frog whole.

At Balgo in Western Australia, the frog is called *ngilapunta*. *Ngila* means slimy and *punta* is the hard lump of sand which indicates the burrowing of the frog, presumably a result of its slime and excretions.

Balgo, Western Australia, 1980

Desert snake

Generally across Australia all snakes are protected. This is because most Australians see them as something to be feared and dispatched immediately with a shovel or other handy implement. Remember that, when you visit the bush, the snake has precedence. If you leave them alone, they won't bother you. Traditionally, some Indigenous peoples ate snake but it is not a dish for most Australians today.

All sorts of snakes can be eaten and in Arnhem Land pythons and file snakes are particularly favoured. However, the particularly venomous, brown snakes are also eaten in some desert regions.

Persuade a friend to track, excavate and kill a large King Brown. While it is still fresh expel the contents of the lower gut by running the finger and thumb down the lower abdomen to the vent. Curl the snake up on hot sand and cover with sand and hot ashes. Cook for about 10 minutes and eat the flesh from the back, avoiding the stomach.

44

Long-necked turtle (*Chelodina rugosa*)

Once again, this is not a choice for non-Indigenous Australians.

This recipe was collected from the Ngarinman people of the western parts of the Victoria River District in the Northern Territory. Their cookbook instructions might go something like this:

> Catch a long-necked turtle on a hook and line — or, traditionally, by diving for it. Break its neck or head to kill it. Make a small incision in the neck and find the windpipe. Cut the windpipe and blow into it filling the lungs with air. Prepare a medium-to-hot fire for cooking. Place the turtle on its back in the fire and heat for about five minutes. Turn the turtle over onto its front and heat through for an additional five minutes. Remove from the fire.
>
> Beat the breast plate with a stout stick until it is broken. Lever off the plate until it is all removed and discard. Take the turtle by the neck and pull it free from the shell. Remove and discard the lower intestines and the bladder. Separate out the other parts, particularly the arms and legs, neck, head, liver and other intestines and the fat. Cook lightly on the ashes. Replace the inverted shell on the fire and cook the rest of the meat, the gravy and any other parts in it. Serve in the shell with the gravy and fat.

Amanbidji station, Northern Territory, 1986

I once worked on a long bush trip with a man who had undertaken to avoid all meat, except fish and snake, while he was in mourning for a relative. Since our resources on the trip were quite limited and, being in the desert, there was no water, let alone any fish, his diet was restricted to snake and tins of sardines. He was quite unwilling to hunt for the snakes himself — by its nature it's a dangerous occupation — preferring that we hunt them for him.

The added incentive for us to do so on his behalf was provided by the atmosphere in the hot and restricted confines of the vehicle cab as we travelled along. The surfeit of sardines presented singular and distinct olfactory disadvantages I can tell you.

Preparing a freshwater turtle for cooking.

Crocodile (*Crocodylus johnstoni*)

There's no recipe here for freshwater crocodile as I have never actually seen one cooked. It is a favourite meat in both the Kimberley and the Top End where it is found. I was once offered a feed of crocodile, out of the boot of a car, where the reptile had been stored after being cooked. Not surprisingly it tasted rather fishy. It was whitish and rather stringy.

Goanna (various species, but particularly *Varanus gouldii*)

The following recipes for goanna are once again traditional ways of preparing food that utilise species that should not be taken by non-Indigenous people. However, the traditional instructions might go something like this:

Failure to gut the goanna properly may have dire consequences. Once, a fierce willy-willy, that damaged buildings at a Western Desert community, was blamed on the fact that a whitefella had caught a goanna and cooked it without gutting it according to Aboriginal law.

Track a goanna and kill it with a stick. Take a small forked twig from a gum tree. Break the stick so it is about fifteen centimetres long. Trim the fork to form a small hooked implement. Insert the hook into the anal aperture of the goanna and twist it lightly. Withdraw the hook extracting the lower intestine in the process. Ensure that the intestine pulls away cleanly from the body of the reptile. No cut should be made in the abdomen of the goanna.

Prepare a fire for cooking and clear an area of sand free of hot ashes. Place the goanna on the hot sand and cover with more hot sand. Put ashes on top of the sand. Cook for about fifteen minutes depending on taste and the size of the goanna.

Jigalong, Western Australia, 1974

Dried goanna

I have not come across many traditional recipes for preserved or dried food. The one that follows may have been the consequence of influence from pastoralists who settled the inland Pilbara region of Western Australia from the 1860s on.

Take a freshly cooked goanna (see above). Pound the meat, including the bones, on a rocky slab with a pebble chopper. Separate out into small pieces and set to dry in the sun. Store by wrapping in paperbark until required.

Yarraloola station, Western Australia, 1980

I was told that meat preserved in this way would keep for months.

Blue-tongue lizard (*Tiliqua multifasciata*)

Extract the lower gut by squeezing the abdomen between the thumb and forefinger or run your thumbnail down the stomach to the vent to expel the contents of the gut. Cook the whole animal lightly in the hot ashes and discard skin, feet and the head. Most of the remainder can be eaten though parts of the intestine may be given to the dogs.

Maralinga Lands, South Australia, 1988

Meat drying on a tree: Wadangine outstation, Pilbarra, Western Australia.

Vegetables

Bush tomatoes

The bush tomato (*solanum*) is still a popular food in desert regions. The fruit is typically small, yellow-green and the size of a small tomato. It grows on a low prickly bush close to the ground. Flowers are usually blue and the leaves are a pale olive-green.

The fruit is first cleaned of all seeds which are very bitter. Cook them in pieces in the ashes of a cool fire. The fruit can also be eaten raw and they make an interesting addition to a salad.

Maralinga Lands, South Australia, 1988

There are a number of other vegetables found in the bush that can be eaten. These include:

- the bush banana (*Leichardtia australis*) known to the southern Pitjantjatjara as *kalkulay* and as *utiralya* or *unturngi* further north. These are consumed raw, or lightly cooked in the ashes, as described above;
- the wild plum (*Santalum lanceolatum*) which is eaten raw; and
- the quandong (*Santalum acuminatum*) or *mangata*. The kernel of the quandong nut was also ground and mixed with water to form a medical dressing.

Both the wild plum and quandong can be reconstituted with water when dried.

Yams

Better known still are the yams of northern Australia which require special treatment to expel toxins. They must be soaked in water, preferably running water, for several days, then sliced and dried in the sun, soaked again and then cooked. This process is not to be undertaken by the inexperienced and readers of this account will be well advised to avoid this food at all costs unless prepared by an Aboriginal or Torres Strait Islander expert.

Lily roots and seed head (*nymphaea* sp)

Pick bulb, stem and seed head of the blue water lily which the Ngarinman know as *kanguni*. The seed head is eaten raw or lightly roasted in the ashes. It tastes like sweet corn. The bulb is cooked in the ashes. The stem is also edible but is considered rather poor and only to be eaten in straitened circumstances. However, it can also be used as a straw for drinking water and acts as an effective filter.

Amanbidji Station, Northern Territory, 1983

Eggs

Turtle eggs

Turtles and their eggs are protected by law.

Many factors have contributed to the decline of turtles, including over-fishing, exploitation for the shell and the grim fact that turtles, like dugongs, get caught in fishing nets and drown. Aboriginal and Torres Strait Islander peoples are today very aware of the necessity to develop a sustainable economy for these and other species so that levels of traditional exploitation can be maintained. What follows is an insight into the importance of the turtle in the traditional economy.

Around the tropical coast of northern Australia turtle eggs have long been a delicacy amongst Indigenous Australians. There are several species of turtle hunted for their food. They lay their eggs in a sand nest dug just above the high-water mark. The female leaves the ocean at high tide, usually under cover of darkness, excavates the nest, lays up to eighty eggs. She covers the eggs and fills in the hole then returns to the sea before the tide recedes too far.

The best time to collect the eggs is in late July or August on Groote Eylandt. I have seen them taken in April on the Wessel Islands off northern Arnhem Land.

Watching a turtle lay her eggs at night on a remote stretch of beach is an experience I will never forget. I am pleased to write that that particular turtle and her eggs remained undisturbed.

The tracks made by the turtle are easy to see when you walk along a beach. However, not all tracks lead to a nest since the turtle may decide the area she has chosen is too hard and rocky to dig. The forager probes the nest site with a stout stick to ascertain whether there are eggs inside before digging. The eggs are like soft ping-pong balls and about the same size and white.

Take fresh turtle eggs and place them in a billy with fresh or salt water. Boil briefly. No amount of cooking will make the white set. Serve individually. The eggs are eaten by biting the skin which is quite soft and sucking the contents out.

Wessel Islands, Northern Territory, 1983

Turtle embryos are also eaten, if the eggs are part developed, in the same manner.

Shorty Wanambi collecting turtle eggs: Groote Eylandt Northern Territory

Birds' eggs

Subject to state and territory laws protecting various species there are a number of eggs that make good eating to be found in the bush.

Indigenous people traditionally ate a number of different eggs, including those of the emu (*Dromaius novae-hollandiae*), the bush turkey (*Ardeotis australis*), the magpie goose (*Anseranas semipalmata*) and the mallee fowl (*Leipoa ocellata*), to name but a few.

Try this technique with a hen's egg or the larger duck's or even a goose egg.

Pierce the egg at one end (an opportunity to make sure that it is not addled) and place upright, hole uppermost in the hot sand and ashes of a cool fire. Leave for about five minutes. Knock off the top of the shell and eat. Obviously, cooking time depends on the size of the egg.

Maralinga Lands, South Australia, 1988

non-Indigenous styles of Australian bush cooking

The following recipes are designed to cater for bush travellers who have a minimum of equipment and are unable to carry fragile or perishable items except for basics like meat and some vegetables. For the most part the recipes assume an ability to carry reasonable quantities of ingredients. Tinned food has been a long-time standby of the bush cook but the quality varies enormously, sometimes being frankly inedible unless you are very hungry. Dried foods can be handy, including powdered soup, meat substitutes, and a whole range of packet foods which are available from camping and outdoor shops.

I have found that there is little substitute for fresh ingredients, even if they are used to augment tinned or dried food. With care, cabbage, potatoes, onions, carrots, garlic, mixed herbs, ginger root and root vegetables can travel quite well for up to a week, without refrigeration, even in hot conditions. Avoid soft green vegetables (except perhaps cabbage), tomatoes, eggs (of course) and most fruit, although oranges are surprisingly resilient. Other ingredients worthy of consideration are stock cubes, powdered sauces, flour and two-minute noodles.

If you are forced to eat tinned food because nothing else is available, remove the lid carefully, leaving one centimetre attached. Taking care not to cut yourself fold the lid back and bend it to form a handle. Place the tin in a hot sand and ash fire but not in the direct flames.

My first trip to the bush was planned for me by a man who taught me much. This trip in Western Australia was remarkable also for the number of tins of food we consumed. The plethora of tins were taken on the assumption that only tins travelled well and would remain fit for eating in hot desert conditions. In fact we took so many tins with us that we could have manufactured several replica sets of Ned Kelly's armour. One night I counted no less than eight tins warming up in the fire. The next morning before departing the camp these empty cans had to be buried. I remember thinking that there had to be a better way. There is.

A friend suggested once, on a trip in the Great Sandy Desert when I was about to heat up a tin for my dinner, that I could save myself a lot of trouble and cut out the middleman altogether if I took the unopened tin and some toilet paper and put them both down in the bush together somewhere discreet, beneath a tree.

I once had a tin of Scottish lobster bisque that a colleague and I saved for the right moment. On a cold, cheerless rainy evening at the old atomic test site at Emu in South Australia, with doubts as to the safety of the camp site and the non-appearance of the group that we were supposed to meet, we decided that this was the time. Despite the rain and damp, we heated the prize tin on the coals. It was excellent. But I had a haunting feeling that we, and the bisque, might have become radioactive.

Occasionally turn the tin around and, if possible, stir the contents. This can be difficult because tins are usually full to the brim. Eat directly from the tin with a spoon.

In recent years the old fashioned tin has been replaced by the ring pull variety obviating the need for a tin opener. But the new design does not consider the needs of the bush cook. Once 'pulled' the top separates from the tin and cannot be used as a handle. I first encountered this difficulty when I camped one wet night in the desert between Kintore and Docker River on the NT/WA border. While I managed the tin with the aid of my pocket handkerchief on that occasion, this technique is not recommended as I burnt several large holes in it in the process. Outdoor equipment stores sell a pot lifter that is handy for these type of tins.

Tins are a matter of experimentation and taste. As a general rule, avoid tinned meals that contain a great deal of salt and huge quantities of indescribable and unidentifiable materials that may or may not have had their origins in vegetable matter. The best value is tinned meat, particularly steak which is also the most expensive. I am ambivalent about corned beef but, if you do buy it, get one hundred per cent beef with no cereal. I am not a great fan of Camp Pie.

Tinned fish is generally good value. I have lived on sardines for lunch for weeks at a time. The taste tends to linger, especially if you have a beard or moustache, and I probably had much in common with my friend mentioned earlier with the food taboo!

Tinned steak and kidney pies, also available in other versions including chicken, are good value and taste pretty good, provided you can learn the trick of how to cook them (see below). There is also a range of so-called gourmet tins some of which are surprisingly good. Though not cheap it is worth having a few for a special occasion.

While tinned food may have to form a part of your diet, the recipes that follow demonstrate that you can either do without them altogether, or use them as a basis for meals that are tasty and nutritious. As a first step make sure you have the following:

tinfoil;

a tin-opener (or your SAK);

matches (of course);

oil;

mixed herbs;

stock cubes;

garlic;

root ginger (lasts almost for ever); and

powdered soup mix.

Provided you have at least some fresh, or reasonably fresh, ingredients you ought to be able to knock up something better than a hot burnt tin of Hawaiian Surprise!

Raw cabbage makes a good accompaniment except, perhaps, at breakfast. Buy a good solid cabbage with plenty of outside leaves as these can be peeled off and discarded later like wrapping when the whole vegetable becomes a little worse for wear. Chop the cabbage finely and add salt and pepper. More advanced preparations include the addition of oil and vinegar or even salad dressing if you have it. For a change try mixing shredded carrot or finely chopped onion with the cabbage (and you have coleslaw). If all else fails plain shredded raw cabbage is very welcome if you haven't had any fresh vegetables for weeks.

Drinks

Cool drinks are never very cool in the bush unless you carry a car fridge. Try soaking an old sock in water. Place the tin in the sock and push it down into the foot. Hang the sock in a tree or from any convenient point and wait till it is only damp. The evaporation of the water from the sock will cause the tin to cool. Tins of fruit can be cooled like this too. They may not be cold but they will taste better when they are not actually warm.

I haven't tested this one yet but I was told that the older and dirtier the sock, the better, because it absorbed water better rather like blotting paper.

Billy tea (method four)

Tea is the drink of the bush. It is easy to make and keeps well, provided you don't get the packet wet. And it is good with or without milk or sugar.

Fill the billy with fresh water and place it on the fire. When the water is boiling shake a good quantity of tea leaves into the palm of your hand. Then, with a pot-lifter handy (see below), throw the leaves into the water, wait no more than two or three seconds and remove the billy from the fire. Allow to stand for three minutes. Swing the billy to settle the leaves or tap the side with a stick several times and watch the leaves sink. Pour and enjoy.

When you open the packet, cut or tear off only a small corner — just sufficient to shake out a small amount. This way, if you knock the packet over, very little will be spilt.

Meat grilled or fried

Pot Lifter
Make a pot lifter by cutting a good stout twig, slightly less than a centimetre thick, from a green branch two centimetres immediately below a small fork. Trim the twig of any other forks and make it about twenty centimetres long. Hold the long part of the pot lifter and hook the fork under the billy wire and lift.

A load of beef: Yandeearra, Western Australia, 1974.

Shovel steak

Find your shovel and clean it by rubbing sand across its face. Build up a good fire and allow it to burn down to hot coals. Place the shovel on the coals, propping the handle on rocks or a box so the shovel blade is more or less flat and the handle is well clear of the flames. Cover the blade with cooking oil and place the steak on the heated surface. Cook to taste.

The shovel can be used to cook any meat and perhaps to fry an egg.

Try cooking an egg in half a grapefruit skin which has had the flesh removed, and eaten. Make sure the grapefruit is set in hot sand and ashes — not on the burning coals. Cook the egg for about five minutes. It tastes a little of the grapefruit but this is not unpleasant.

Chops on the griller

Prepare a hot fire of coals and allow to burn down. The heat is critical as fat from the meat will drip onto the coals and if they are too hot will flare up and burn the meat.

Drink two cans of beer and keep the cans. Find a small rock or drink a third can. Place two of the empty cans in the fire, end up to form a rest for the griller (details on the use of a griller are given in the section on the Bush Kitchen p. 14). Position the rock, or the third can, to support the handle.

Place the lamb chops in the griller and press it closed, fastening the wire together with the clip provided on the handle. Set the griller on the fire resting it on the cans. Turn it over after five or six minutes tending the coals to ensure they remain hot but do not flare up.

This method can be used to cook steak, sausages and many other forms of meat.

Try putting a small bunch of green gumleaves on the fire under the griller. The smoke imparts a distinctive flavour to the meat. It is well worth trying.

I knew a man once whose daughter, working in London, keenly missed the Australian bush. Every year at Christmas he sent her, packed in a jiffy bag, a bundle of gumleaves so that she and her friends could enjoy the smell of the eucalypt on the yuletide fire.

55

Meat on the coals

If you don't have a shovel, a griller or a pan, you can cook your meat directly on the coals. Read the section on Fire in the chapter about the Bush Kitchen on page 17. It is probably best not to start off with a piece of really expensive scotch fillet as your first attempts may not be edible!

A carefully constructed fire is of the utmost importance.

Bury your rubbish! Burn tins out in the fire. This removes traces of food and also ensures that the tins break down faster in the soil or sand. Flatten them with a shovel or hammer. Dig a good deep hole at least thirty centimetres deep — the deeper, the better — and compact the rubbish in the hole. Cover it over with soil. If you bury food scraps make sure they are deep in the ground as foxes or dingoes will go to surprising lengths to dig up your rubbish. If at all possible, take your rubbish home with you, especially any plastic.

Prepare a bed of hot coals, comprising small pieces of slightly glowing charcoal, with no flame and no red-hot pieces on the top of the bed. Avoid ash. Lay the steak carefully on the coals and turn regularly. When cooked remove from the fire and beat with a stick or leaves to remove any ash or charcoal sticking to the meat.

Kebabs

You really need a steel skewer for this although you can try with wooden sticks if you can find some that are long and straight enough. It is also best to use a green stick as it will be less likely to burn. Wooden skewers soaked in water for several hours are less likely to burn before the cooking is finished.

Cut beef or lamb into small cubes. Cut onion into quarters and green pepper into pieces about the size of a large postage stamp. Thread meat, onion and pepper onto the skewer, brush with oil and season. Cook on a medium-to-hot fire of coals. Turn the skewers occasionally.

I worked on many cattle stations where beef is much eaten, but the facilities for killing are limited. Here the procedure for butchering is generally the reverse of standard practice (apart from the initial bullet, that is). After the beast has been killed it is first butchered, then gutted and finally skinned as required.

The initial killing involves a good deal of chasing, unless a suitable beast is in the yard at mustering time. I have bounced over black soil plains in pursuit of the marked 'killer' usually a steer or barren heifer — though how these fellas know it is barren I never worked out. My companions leaned out of the window or hung perilously from the back of the truck. When we came within range a volley of bullets raked the spear grass. Eventually the beast was cornered or bailed up and was shot with a single bullet between the eyes.

What you require next is a sharp knife and an axe and a stout stomach. The technique is to sever the various limbs and remove for later skinning and further division. The stomach is cut open and the breastbone cut to the throat with an axe and the ribs removed. The choice cuts from the rump are taken with the legs, if possible, and the rest is a matter of expediency, convenience and what the truck is capable of carrying back to camp. I once had eight people, two 200-litre drums of fuel, and camping and other gear on the back of a Toyota, when my companions decided we needed some meat. A butchered bovine weighs a great deal and we had to leave some behind. The capacity of a Toyota never ceases to amaze me.

Tinfoil dinners

Tinfoil is the most useful cooking item for the bush cook. It is relatively cheap. It is effective. It requires no washing up. But don't throw it on the fire when you have finished with it because it won't burn. After you have gone, and the ashes of your fire have blown away, the foil will still be there. Burn it off to remove traces of food and either take it home with you or bury it at least thirty centimetres in the ground.

Fish in foil

Place a fish fillet, or a whole fish if you prefer, on foil and turn up the edges to form a dish. Squeeze lemon onto the fish and add mixed herbs, salt and pepper and a quarter of a cup of water (use sea water if you are by the sea). Fold over the foil and seal the edges, making sure that the foil is secure. Carefully place the foil parcel onto a hot bed of sand and ashes, cover with the hot sand, ashes and then coals. Leave to cook for about twenty minutes depending on the size of the fish. Carefully remove the foil package from the fire and set it on a clean rock or other convenient surface. Dust off the sand, ash and any charcoal with a brush made of leaves. Blow on the crimped edges of the parcel to remove all traces of dust. Open the foil and serve.

Steak and kidney pie

There is a proprietary brand of pie produced in a flat tin dish with a sealed top. Inside there is uncooked pastry encasing the meat filling. The pie represents good value for money and is quite delicious. The major problem is the pastry that needs to be cooked.

Open the tin and remove the lid completely. Take a piece of tinfoil generously larger than the surface area of the tin. Pour a little oil on the foil and smear it with your finger. Place the foil, oiled side down, onto the pastry and wrap the foil loosely round the sides. Make sure that the foil is not too tight but securely seals the pie dish. Place the tin onto a hot bed of sand and ashes. Cover the foil with hot sand, ashes and finally hot coals. The latter must not come into direct contact with the foil otherwise the pastry will burn.

Cook for about twenty minutes. You may need to replenish the hot coals over the cooking pie to ensure consistency of heat. Unfortunately, there is no sure way of timing the cooking, since much depends on the heat of the fire. However, the pastry should be well cooked, not burnt, and the filling piping hot.

A sea eagle dropped a flathead at my feet once on a beach in the Dampier Archipelago, Western Australia. I had watched him swoop across the surf to pick up his prize and climb heavily with a good sized fish in his talons. As the eagle circled above the fish must have slipped from his grasp and fell to the beach where I quickly retrieved it before the eagle had time to recover it. I hid the fish in a rock crevice away from the ants and a rather angry eagle and picked it up after my day's work, and cooked it for my tea.

58

Remove the pie, foil intact, from the fire. A shovel is the best tool to use. Exercise great caution as any puncture to the foil especially on top will result in grit getting into the meal. Brush off as much sand, ash and charcoal as possible, then blow the tinfoil clean. Lift the foil from beneath the pie tin, trying to shed any remaining dust away from the crusty pastry beneath. Eat from the pie tin which, afterwards, makes a useful dish for the dog.

Potatoes in their jackets

Take a clean potato at least the size of your fist. Carefully wrap it in foil. Place it in the hot ashes of a moderate fire and cover with hot sand and then coals. Cook for twenty minutes, turning it after ten minutes. Remove from the fire and brush off surplus ash and sand, blowing on the folds of the foil to ensure all grit is removed. Cut the potato open and make a slash down the centre of each half. Fill with cottage cheese, butter, salt, pepper and creamed corn.

It's quite easy to cook a potato without foil but the temperature of the fire is more critical. You need to be very careful about the ratio of hot sand and ash to burning coals otherwise the potato will be burnt on the outside and raw in the middle. Obviously, without foil, the spud is more likely to be gritty. A smooth-skinned potato, brushed clean, can produce a surprisingly grit-free product.

Onions, carrots, parsnips in foil

Onions can be done like potatoes but they don't need to cook for as long. Carrots and parsnips are tricky as they tend to dry out. It's best to cut them in half and place the thin end with the fat end. Add a little water to the foil and cook for about fifteen minutes. I haven't tried zucchini but I see no reason why this method shouldn't work provided you don't cook them for too long.

One-pan dinners

Mince and cabbage

Slice an onion and fry till golden-brown with a pinch of mixed herbs. Add minced meat, use the tinned variety if necessary, and cook. Shred a cabbage and add to the onion and mince. Season; add garlic to taste and soy sauce if desired. Serve with a baked potato.

Stir-fried vegetables

Should you be in the fortunate position of having lots of vegetables try stir-frying them in a pan, camp oven or a wok if you've brought one. This is an easy and appetising meal and as an added bonus is full of fibre and very good for you.

Chop onion, capsicum, mushrooms, carrots, zucchini, cauliflower, cabbage, and just about any other vegetable you have managed to carry or has survived. Fry the onion with mixed herbs and garlic. Add finely chopped ginger. Add the carrots and cauliflower and any heavier vegetables first, leaving the zucchini, mushroom and cabbage to last. Add soy sauce, a stock cube or even a powdered instant soup mix for taste. Do not overcook. Serve with rice if you can manage it.

Red lentils for breakfast

Breakfast in the bush is best managed with dried food, like muesli or cereals, with powdered or tinned milk and maybe tinned fruit. You should also try UHT milk which comes in stout cartons and will last almost indefinitely unopened. However, once opened, it needs to be used and it doesn't travel well in any case. The following recipe was given to me by a colleague and may be used for breakfast or almost any other meal. It might be best, however, not to eat it before a long day in a cramped Toyota with several other passengers.

Pour red lentils onto a plate and search through them to remove any hard bits — you are probably a long way from any dentists! Place in a billy with water and set on a moderate heat. Add two chicken stock cubes and a green or red pepper, sliced very thin, with crushed garlic or diced onions, or both, to taste. When the lentils are soft, remove from the heat and serve. Getting the right amount of water in the billy initially is important otherwise the soup will be too thin.

Kim Barber, Keep River National Park, Northern Territory, 1997

Bush stew

Bush stew is a concept rather than a recipe although some would argue that it is a way of life. It can be made from more or less anything and is an excellent way of making tinned food palatable which otherwise would remain in the tuckerbox or on the supermarket shelf. The basic rule is that a stew improves in direct proportion to the number of fresh, or relatively fresh, ingredients you supply. A tin of meat, vegetables or soup, with a fresh onion, garlic, mixed herbs, a stock cube and a potato, thrown in for good measure, makes a much better meal than the heated-up contents of a tin.

Always start with an onion fried in the bottom of the camp oven with garlic and mixed herbs. Add fresh meat, if you have it, or use a tin if you do not (see comments on tinned meat and 'meat' above). Add vegetables, including potato, carrots and parsnips, if available. Stir till heated through. Add stock, in the form of a dissolved stock cube, powdered soup mix or, failing all else, just water. Season. Cook for as long as possible, stirring occasionally to make sure the stew doesn't stick to the bottom. Thicken with a little flour, or cornflour, pre-mixed with water if you like, just before serving.

Bubble Bubble stew

A colleague once abandoned me on the banks of the Bubble Bubble Creek, not far from the Keep River National Park in the Northern Territory. In his tuckerbox — an old cardboard box much the worse for wear — I found a piece of ginger, a few potatoes, a carrot, a sorry green pepper, a few stock cubes and a packet of instant noodles. These I transformed into Bubble Bubble stew. He returned just as I was serving up.

Peel a potato, one for each person, and carrot. Thinly slice fresh ginger and place together in a billy over a moderate heat. Bring to the boil, adding a stock cube and a diced green pepper. When the potato and carrot are more or less cooked, add a packet of two-minute noodles, along with the flavouring sachet, if you wish. Remove from the heat when the noodles are soft. Serve.

The trick is to make sure there's not too much water initially as this will form the gravy for the dish which is spoilt if it is too thin and runny. There is a variation of this recipe I call Bucket Stew (not because you make it in a bucket but because I first cooked it at Bucket Springs, also close to the Keep River National Park). For Bucket Stew you add beef cut into cubes. When I tried this I ended up discarding the beef — it was very tough, like the galah. I think the stew would also taste quite good with fish but I haven't tried it.

Curry

The above recipe for bush stew can be used as a basis for a humble curry. Bush curry is typically hot. This is probably due to a lack of other and more subtle curry flavours that are usually beyond the scope of the bush cook. Basic curry powder can transform a stew made mostly from tinned ingredients. However, you can curry fish, meat, vegetables or even eggs and obtain an excellent result. If you are able to carry a small jar of more expensive curry paste you will, perhaps, obtain a richer variety of subtle flavours.

Add the curry paste or powder to the meat and always cook the curry for at least one hour on a low heat, but the longer, the better.

Brown rice and tuna

Cook brown rice in a billy until soft. Drain and add a tin of tuna. Stir over a low heat until the mixture is hot. Serve.

This is an easy meal but the brown rice takes some cooking. Some people think it is never cooked. You can use white long-grained rice if you prefer. A chopped onion added to the rice about five minutes before the rice is cooked gives the mixture more flavour and texture.

The main disadvantage of the dish is that you have to clean the billy before you can make the tea.

Risotto

This might be a little adventurous for many bush cooks but it requires only one pan and most ingredients should be readily available.

> Chop an onion and fry in oil until golden-brown. Add garlic and mixed herbs. Prepare and add minced meat, bacon pieces, chicken livers (these you are unlikely to have) or any other tasty meat pieces. A tinned product optimistically called 'Savoury Mince' could be used. Cook till the meat is tender, or hot. Add one-third of a cup of white rice for each person. Fry the rice, turning it rapidly to prevent sticking, until it is brown. Then add stock, in the form of a stock cube dissolved in hot water, to cover the rice and other ingredients. Cook slowly, stirring occasionally to make sure that the rice does not stick. You may need to add more water or stock as the rice soaks up the liquid quickly. After about fifteen minutes the rice should be cooked. Remove from the heat and serve.

Spaghetti marinara

In the unlikely event that you have access to fresh seafood this is an easy recipe that once again requires only one dish. There are a number of tins on the market containing mixed seafood which can be used for this recipe when fresh seafood is not available.

> Place spaghetti in rapidly boiling water and cook for twelve minutes. Drain. Add a small tin of seafood mixture, season and reheat, stirring the seafood thoroughly in with the spaghetti.
>
> A variation, which requires two pans, involves frying a chopped onion in oil with mixed herbs and a small amount of ginger. Add the seafood mixture and heat through. This mixture is then combined with the cooked spaghetti.

Two-pan dinners

Classic spaghetti bolognaise

Chop an onion and fry in garlic and butter till golden-brown. Add minced meat and cook through. Stir in a tub of tomato puree and/or a tin of tomatoes. Add a bay leaf if you remembered to bring one, salt, pepper and mixed herbs to taste. When the mixture is cooked, prepare stock by dissolving a stock cube in hot water and add to the pan. Stir and simmer for at least twenty minutes.

Cook the spaghetti in a separate billy, boiling for about twelve minutes or less until it is *al dente,* if that is the way you prefer it. Serve the spaghetti on a plate with the bolognaise sauce poured over the top. Sprinkle with parmesan cheese.

Chicken with Kingsley's wine sauce

Dice chicken and cook in hot oil with mixed herbs. Remove from the heat and fry an onion in the same pan, with garlic and seasoning. Add mushrooms and sauté. Return the chicken to the pan and heat. Add two teaspoons of green peppercorns and a glass of white wine. Cook through. Thicken the stock with one spoonful of cornflour, pre-mixed with a little cold water. Stir thoroughly and serve on a bed of rice.

Andrew Collett and Geoff Eames cooking lunch: Maralinga Lands during preparation for the Royal Commission into British Nuclear Testing in Australia, 1985.

Apricot chicken

Pan-fry chicken drumsticks or other cuts in the camp oven until golden brown. Pour a tin of apricot nectar over the chicken and place half a dozen prunes round the meat. Add water, if necessary, and cook in a medium fire for about 45 minutes or until the chicken is cooked, stirring occasionally. Serve with potatoes or rice.

Try to make sure that someone else has the task of cleaning the camp oven.

Eiffel chicken

This is a variation on apricot chicken and is simpler.

Pan-fry onions in the camp oven until brown and then add the chicken. Mix a packet of dried French onion soup with about half a mug of cold water. Pour the soup mix over the meat and onions and allow to simmer for about half an hour adding more water if required.

You can use most soup mixes for this recipe, but French onion provides the tastiest mix in my view. Once again try to convince the diners that the cook doesn't do the washing up.

Lemon chicken

Cut a medium onion into rings and fry in hot oil with garlic and mixed herbs until golden-brown. Dice the chicken and add, cooking until white. Take the juice of two lemons and add about half a cup of hot water and two teaspoons of brown sugar, to taste. Cut four slices from a third lemon and reserve for garnish. If you have a grater, grate the rind otherwise finely chop the remaining lemon peel and set to one side. Add the lemon juice, water and sugar mixture to the pan and simmer well. Add the grated or finely chopped peel and stir in. Finally, thicken with a little flour or cornflour, if desired. Garnish with the four lemon slices and serve when they are heated through.

It is important not to overcook the rind as it tends to lose its flavour and get lost, so the last stages of the recipe must be done quickly, just before serving.

Chicken curry and yoghurt

You can make a paste from curry powder, oil, pepper and any other ingredients that take your fancy. Pan-fry an onion with garlic and mixed herbs. Take chicken pieces and smear liberally with the curry paste. Fry the chicken until golden-brown and cooked throughout. Add a liberal serve of plain yoghurt and a handful of chopped almonds. Cook until the yoghurt is well mixed with the chicken, onions and almonds. Remove and serve with rice.

Fettuccine

This is a great stand by and, although it requires two pans, is easy to prepare and is adaptable. You can use just about any available ingredients including tinned foods. The version presented here is my favourite but does require fresh ingredients.

Chop an onion and fry in butter, oil or margarine, with several cloves of garlic and mixed herbs. Add mushrooms and any other vegetables, finely chopped. Take two rashers of bacon, and remove the rind and any excess fat. Cut into small pieces and fry with the other ingredients. Add olive paste, or pitted olives, sundried tomatoes, fresh coriander — dried or bottled will do if no fresh coriander is available — and cook well.

Add fettuccine to rapidly boiling water and cook for six minutes. Remove and drain and set to one side. Allow any excess fat to drain from the cooked mixture before spooning it into the fettuccine and adding generous quantities of grated parmesan cheese. Place on a low heat and stir rapidly for about five minutes or until the cheese is all melted and the fettuccine and mixture are well integrated. Serve with grated parmesan cheese sprinkled on top. You can try adding tinned cream to the final mixture for a really rich result, if your liver is up to it.

Akerman's Kimberley kangaroo

Kangaroo is available in many supermarkets so you don't have to go and shoot your own — in fact, it's best that you don't! Since kangaroo is something of a national dish try this recipe given to me by an old friend, Kim Akerman.

Use at least one kangaroo fillet per person. Slice the fillets into two centimetre thick sections. Rub with a mild chilli paste. Brown fillets in oil in a frying pan, then take off the heat. Skin some ripe mangoes and slice. Lay the slices on top of the kangaroo fillets. Replace on the heat and gently cook until the mango is reduced to a puree and the fillets poach in the liquid. Serve hot with jasmine rice and snowpeas or the nearest equivalent.

Author's beef ration: Yandeearra Station, Western Australia. 1974.

Afters

Confectionery

Not very enterprising, but confectionery is a great standby for difficult times. Choose the non-melting type, such as muesli bars, but check the use-by date in outback stores! A note of caution, my dentist tells me that muesli bars are in the top three tooth breakers!

More tins

The Aboriginal people of south eastern Australia ate bogong moths taken from the high country and lightly roasted in the fire.

I've never tried them nor have I come across any other Indigenous recipes that use moths. However, it set me thinking about the Tiger Moth and some tinned delights enthusiastically espoused by an old bush pilot.

The Tiger Moth was the aeroplane of choice for Don McCaskill, a man of the cloth I was privileged to know who had spent many years bashing round the Gascoyne region of Western Australia. As a flying clergyman he had visited many remote properties in his Tiger Moth and had been something of a pioneer in the region. I was lucky enough to do one big trip with him down the Canning Stock Route by four-wheel drive, not as it happens in a Tiger Moth. Don's favourite bush tucker was cold tinned rice cream that to my mind had all of the disadvantages of rice pudding and none of the advantages. It certainly made catering for him easy.

Don was the only man I ever met who had a mouse in his Landrover. I think it took up residence when he left the vehicle for several weeks when he returned to Perth on holiday. He even had a mouse trap to try and catch it but the mouse was too good for him. It was a brave mouse that survived the Canning Stock Route I can tell you.

On that trip, in heavy sandhill country, he blew a core plug in the engine block of his old Landrover. We stopped to repair it with Araldite and I remember he told me how he used to fly across the Murchison in his Tiger Moth. Sometimes, when the head wind was very strong and he was following the northern inland highway, he would watch vehicles hundreds of feet below him overtake his slow plane.

Being a clergyman, of course, I never doubted the veracity of his stories and they were always entertaining. He went on to describe how once, high above the Gascoyne, the propeller fell off his plane and helicoptered to the ground.

Alarmed, but not unduly worried, he circled and glided to a clearing where he landed, not too far from where he saw the propeller fall. He got out of the plane and searched the bush until he found the prop largely undamaged but a little chipped. He carried it back to the plane and, with his bush tool kit, bolted it back in place. Making sure the bolts were really tight, he started the engine, taxied and resumed his journey. The Araldite was the quick-drying variety, so by the time it occurred to me to probe the details of the story, the glue had hardened and it was time for us to resume our trip.

In proud memory of Don, I give you:

Rice cream surprise

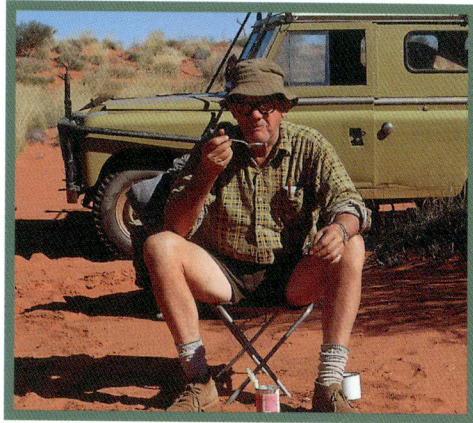

Don McCaskill eating rice cream

Take a slightly warm tin of rice cream preferably one that has travelled for at least two weeks. Open with care retaining a portion of the lid as a handle. Sprinkle lightly with sugar. Consume seated on a box, drum or camp stool. After eating some of the contents add tinned fruit and syrup for taste.

Self-saucing puddings

Some tins of self-saucing puddings are heated in boiling water without removing the top. While this works (that is, the tin doesn't explode), make sure the billy doesn't boil dry as the tin will then certainly explode.

An alternative is to partially-remove the tin lid and fold it back to form a handle. Place the tin in the hot ashes turning occasionally to make sure it doesn't burn. The contents will bubble a little as the sauce cooks and the pudding heats through. Serve in a dish, with the sauce equally distributed, and add a generous serve of tinned cream, if you dare.

Humble tinned fruit

Probably the best stand by. First cool the tin in a wet sock suspended in a tree then combine the fruit with a small tin of cream. I particularly enjoy grapefruit and apricots in hot weather although satsuma plums are a great favourite too, as I've already noted.

Baked and fried puds

Apart from tinned desserts like rice cream, self-saucing pud and fruit, there's not much scope for the bush cook without an oven, dedication and boundless enthusiasm. However, the following recipes provide an insight into the gastronomic delights that are possible in ideal circumstances. Two obvious methods require fundamentals already discussed: the humble frying pan or shovel; and direct baking in the coals.

There is a proprietary brand of tinned cream on the market that comes in small tins and is quite edible. Keep a few tins handy for these desserts.

Crepe sundown

This is really a thin version of the pancakes described earlier in the Breads section of the Indigenous Bush recipes.

> Make a batter mix with flour, water and eggs. Allow to stand. Use the camp oven or a heavy frying pan. Add oil to the pan and heat until it is hot but not burning. Quickly pour a thin layer of mixture into the pan and cook quickly. Remove and place to one side while cooking the remainder. Serve with sugar and lemon juice, or roll with a filling of strawberry jam, marmalade or pieces of tinned fruit.

Fruit fritters

This is a great stand by and may be easier than crepes. However, fritters are fried and tend to be fatty.

> Choose some fruit. Bananas, although they travel very badly, are probably the best because they don't need much cooking. Apples, pears and even tropical fruits can be used. Make a batter mix and heat oil in a pan. Batter the fruit and pan-fry rapidly turning just once. Serve with sugar, lemon juice or cream to taste.

Banana decadence

> Take a firm banana and puncture the skin in several places, making holes large enough to take pieces of chocolate or chocolate chips that should be forced into the flesh of the fruit. Wrap in foil and cook slowly in warm sand and ashes for about ten to fifteen minutes. Remove from the fire and unwrap. Serve with extra chocolate, tinned cream or fruit.

You can cook the banana directly in the ashes but the sand and ash will probably adhere hopelessly to the banana and chocolate mix that tends to ooze from the fruit.

Baked apples Cairo style

Using your Swiss Army Knife, carefully core a firm cooking apple and fill it with nuts and dates. Wrap in foil and bake in the ashes. When cooked serve with cream, milk and sugar.

Topless oranges

Cut the top off an orange and prod contents with a knife or spoon. Drain off some of the juice and replace with plenty of sugar and liqueur (use brandy, Grand Marnier, etc) or, in the event that such is not to be had, whisky or (as a last resort) rum. Replace the lid and cook slowly in warm sand and ashes for about twenty minutes or until soft inside. Serve in the peel.

Orange tango

Peel and dice oranges and discard the peel and pith. Steep in a little water in the camp oven with sugar added and the liqueur of your choice (or whisky or rum if you prefer). Stew slowly for about half an hour or until the fruit is soft. Serve with additional sugar, and liqueur, to taste, with the juice poured over the top.

Bush camp and a Swan Lager beer can.

And to finish–
Liqueur and an after-dinner mint

The Canning Stock Route in Western Australia runs roughly from
Wiluna, north and east through the heart of the Great Sandy Desert, to
Halls Creek in the Kimberley. While the northern and southern sections
are through station country the middle sections are a gruelling series of
unmitigated sand dunes. The rough track, devoid of habitation and for
the most part water, weaves between the dunes doubling or tripling the
distance between the old wells, many of which are now in disrepair and
some of which lie many bone-jolting kilometres off the track. A journey
along the Stock Route remains a serious undertaking. As several
different Aboriginal groups own the country formal permission is
required from each to undertake the trip.

I did a major trip down the Stock Route in 1976 with a valued colleague
called Charles and some Aboriginal men from Balgo, a former Palatine
mission and now a community on the northern fringes of the Great
Sandy Desert. The trip stretched my resources in basic bush cooking.
Charles claimed to be something of a connoisseur, particularly of
spirituous liquors. He had rung me just before I left Derby en route for
the bush, and asked if I would please bring a bottle of something to
soothe our weary bones at the end of the day. Into Dalgety's store I went
and bought a bottle of Bundaberg rum.

During the next couple of weeks, while we pitted our wits against the
never-ending sand dunes of the Stock Route, the rum was consumed,
under the stars, in modest sips from our enamel mugs. Bone weary and
usually quite late, when the chores were done and the field notes written
up, we sat in the dark by the flickering light of a small fire and toasted
our progress. It provided a relaxing end to an otherwise challenging day.
I don't remember how long the rum lasted, but I think between us and
with our moderate appetites, it was most of the trip.

For certain it was always dark when I poured us a dram and Charles
never saw the bottle in daylight. On several occasions he pointed out to
me how excellent was the taste of the liquor. He never commented on
the variety or the brand.

After the expedition was over and we had packed and farewelled our companions, I finally left Charles in Derby while I returned to the Pilbara for some other business. As we parted, he mentioned the bottle I had provided and thanked me for my generosity. 'Not before time', I replied. 'And next time, Charles, you can shout the treat.' There was a slight pause before he added as a parting shot, 'Next time, can you buy some Bundaberg rum instead of that brandy you brought along on this trip? I've never been that keen on brandy!' Alas, I was already part-way down the road by the time the implications of his statement sunk in. And it hadn't been a cheap bottle either.

The night has had other tricks in store in the bush.

While I have never been in the position to take advantage of an after-dinner mint, I have had an after-dinner muesli bar. A community storeman once gave me a whole box of muesli bars as sustenance on a trip I did into the Little Sandy Desert. They were good to eat at night after dinner. So, I consumed well over half of them in the dark not able to see what I was eating and, like Charles, I was more concerned with the taste than with the variety. For some reason it was several days, and several bars, later that I decided to eat one in daylight. I noted to my horror that it was full of weevil maggots. It's very dark at night in the bush and you soon forget how dependent you become on electric light.

Discussions about the protection of sacred sites at Sandy Billabong, Noonkenbah Station, Kimberley, Western Australia. Nipper Tabagee (centre) and Dickey Skinner (seated on the bull bar) and two other men from the Noonkenbah stockcamp, August 1978

73

I guess the bars were well past their use-by date although such concepts did not exist in those days which is why the storeman had given them away.

On 14 July 1976 I noted in my diary:

...fuelled up and arsed about, still some last-minute fixing to do, and so off about 4.30 pm. Drove without incident to the other side of Nullagine where camped the night. Some cloud, with a few drops of rain...

I remember that night there were dingoes howling round my camp.

When dinner is eaten, I've needed no excuse to stretch out under the stars of a northern Australian night to watch a lonely satellite be drawn across the sky by an invisible insistent thread.

Night may have its disadvantages for connoisseurs of fine spirits and muesli bars but it reveals far more than the brightest daylight. The panoply of the night is the exposure of the whole universe laid open to your view. How many people have the opportunity to share this view, uninterrupted, beyond the sound even of the infernal combustion engine? It's yours for the taking in Australia. Enjoy it, honour it, and protect it.

And if the recipes contained in this little book help you to settle back on your swag and enjoy the greatest show on earth then I have added something. For of all the great joys of life, travel is one and good eating is another; while the opportunity to appreciate great untrammelled vistas is certainly another.

Good travelling, great eating and may you share many happy star-filled nights in the great Australian bush.

Settling in for the night, Maralinga Lands, Great Victoria Desert, South Australia, 1982.

Index

A

Amanbidji Station,
    Northern Territory, 45, 48

B

Balgo, Western Australia, 9, 28, 44, 72
barbecue plate, 14
billy, 11–12, 27–28, 39, 50, 54, 61–64
black-lipped oysters, 41
blue-tongue lizard (*Tiliqua multifasciata*), 47
bucket, 24
budgerigar (*Melopsittacus undulatus*), 40
bush banana (*leichardtia australis*), 48
bush turkey (*Ardeotis australis*), 34, 50
bushfire, 18

C

camp grill, 14
camp site, 17
camp stretcher, 22
campfire, *see fire*
crocodile (*Crocodylus johnstoni*), 46
curry, 62, 66

D

damper, 29–30
desert frogs (*Notoden nichollsi* Parker), 43–44
desert snake, 44
drinks, 26–27, 53

E

echidna or porcupine (spiny anteater)
    (*Tachyglossus aculeatus*), 37
eggs, 9, 49, 51, 62
emu (*Dromaius novae-hollandiae*), 36, 50

F

feral cat (*Felix domestica*), 39
fire, 12, 16–22
fish, reptiles and other meat, 40
freshwater mussels, 42
frying pan, 14–15, 30, 67

G

galah (*Cacatua roseicapilla*), 39
Galiwinku, Arnhem Land, 41
goanna (particularly *Varanus gouldii*), 46–47
goat moth (*Cossidae*), 42
Great Sandy Desert, 9, 52
Great Victoria Desert, 20, 38
Groote Eylandt, 40–41, 49

J

Jigalong, Western Australia, 46

K

kangaroo, 9, 23, 31–33, 67
Keep River National Park, Northern
    Territory, 61–62
Kimberley, 34, 46

L

local fire regulations, 18
long-necked turtle (*Chelodina rugosa*), 45

M

magpie goose (*Anseranas semipalmata*), 50
mallee fowl (*Leipoa ocellata*), 50
Maralinga Lands, South Australia, 28, 30–31, 36, 39, 43, 47, 50
mulga, 19

N

native title rights, 23
natural environment, 22
Ngarinman, 45, 48

P

packet food, 51
Pilbara, 36, 40, 46
Pitjantjatjara, 18, 20, 31, 36, 37, 47
pot lifter, 52, 54
preparation areas, 17
protected species, 4, 27, 35, 37–38, 43–46, 49

Q

quandong (*santalum acuminatum*), 48

R

red kangaroo (*Macropus rufus*), 31–32

S

sandstorms, 21
shade, 17
shovel, 15, 37, 44, 55–56, 70
sleeping areas, 22
snakes, 22, 44, 45
stingray, 40–41
sun, 17, 47–48
swag, 20, 22, 74
Swiss Army Knife (SAK), 12

T

table, 7, 17, 22, 24
tinned food, fruit and meat, 51–52, 61, 66
turtle eggs, 49–50

U

utensils,7–9, 11–15, 17, 21

V

vegetables, 33, 47–48, 51, 53, 60–62, 66
vehicles, 17, 68
Victoria River District, 45

W

water, 8, 12, 15–17, 21
waterbags and containers, 15–17, 21
Wessel Islands, Northern Territory, 40–41, 49–50
wet season, 19
wild plum (*santalum lanceolatum*), 48
wind, 17–18, 21–22
windbreak, 11–22
wire, 12–14, 24
    witchetty grubs (*Xyleutes leucomochla*), 42
wombat (*Lasiorhinus latifrons*), 24, 38
wood, 18–19, 21

Y

Yalata, South Australia, 31–33
yams, 48
Yarraloola station, Western Australia, 47

Recipes

Indigenous Bush Recipes 27

Drinks 27
  Billy tea (method 1) 27
  Billy tea (method 2) 28
  Sweet sugar lerp 28
  Sweet nectar 29

Breads 29
  Damper 29
  Fat fella tucker 30
  Pancakes 31
  Bush twist 31

Meat 31
  Kangaroo 32
  Bush turkey (*Ardeotis australis*) 35
  Emu (*Dromaius novae-hollandiae*) 36
  Echidna or porcupine (spiny anteater)(*Tachyglossus aculeatus*) 37
  Wombat (*Lasiorhinus latifrons*) 38
  Galah (*Cacatua roseicapilla*) 39
  Budgerigar (*Melopsittacus undulatus*) 40

Fish, reptiles and other meat 40
  Stingray fish balls 40
  Black-lipped oysters 41
  Freshwater mussels 42
  Witchetty grubs (*Xyleutes leucomochla*) 42
  Desert frogs (*Notoden nichollsi Parker*) 43
  Frog 44
  Desert snake 44
  Long-necked turtle (*Chelodina rugosa*) 45
  Goanna (various species, but particularly *Varanus gouldii*) 46
  Dried goanna 46

Blue-tongue lizard (*Tiliqua multifasciata*) 47

Vegetables 47
  Bush tomatoes 47
  Yams 48
  Lily roots and seed head (*nymphaea sp*) 48

Eggs 49
  Turtle eggs 49
  Birds' eggs 50

Non-Indigenous styles of Australian Bush Cooking 51

Drinks 53
  Billy tea 54

Meat grilled or fried 54
  Shovel steak 55
  Chops on the griller 55
  Meat on the coals 56
  Kebabs 56

Tinfoil dinners 57
Fish in foil 58
Steak and kidney pie 58
Potatoes in their jackets 59
Onions, carrots, parsnips in foil 59

One-pan dinners 60
  Mince and cabbage 60
  Stir-fried vegetables 60
  Red lentils for breakfast 60
  Bush stew 61
  Bubble Bubble stew 61
  Curry 62
  Brown rice and tuna 62
  Risotto 63
  Spaghetti marinara 63
Two-pan dinners 64
  Classic spaghetti bolognaise 64
  Chicken with Kingsley's wine sauce 64
  Apricot chicken 65

Eiffel chicken 65
Lemon chicken 65
Chicken curry and yoghurt 66
Fettuccine 66
Akerman's Kimberley kangaroo 67

Afters 67
Confectionery 67
More tins 67
Rice cream surprise 69
Self-saucing puddings 69
Humble tinned fruit 69

Baked and fried puds 69
Crepe sundown 70
Fruit fritters 70
Banana decadence 70
Baked apples Cairo style 71
Topless oranges 71
Orange tango 71

Notes